With love
from
Gerry & Sheila

Christmas '88.

Hope you get as
much support from
this as I do from
my copy — Gerry

INSPIRING MESSAGES
FOR DAILY LIVING

Cedar books by Norman Vicent Peale

THE POWER OF POSITIVE THINKING
THE POWER OF POSITIVE THINKING FOR YOUNG PEOPLE
THE AMAZING RESULTS OF POSITIVE THINKING
THE POSITIVE PRINCIPLE TODAY
THE POSITIVE WAY TO CHANGE YOUR LIFE
ENTHUSIASM MAKES THE DIFFERENCE
A GUIDE TO CONFIDENT LIVING
STAY ALIVE ALL YOUR LIFE
THE TOUGH-MINDED OPTIMIST
UNLOCK YOUR FAITH-POWER
THE NEW ART OF LIVING
THE JOY OF POSITIVE LIVING
POSITIVE THOUGHTS FOR THE DAY
YOU CAN IF YOU THINK YOU CAN

with Dr Smiley Blanton:

THE ART OF REAL HAPPINESS
FAITH IS THE ANSWER

Inspiring Messages
For
Daily Living

NORMAN VINCENT PEALE

CEDAR

An imprint of William Heinemann Limited

Published by Cedar Books
an imprint of
William Heinemann Limited
10 Upper Grosvenor Street, London W1X 9PA
LONDON   MELBOURNE
JOHANNESBURG   AUCKLAND

Copyright © 1956 by Norman Vincent Peale

First published as a Cedar Book 1959
This impression 1988

0 434 11107 4

Printed in Great Britain by
Richard Clay Ltd, Bungay, Suffolk

The techniques and principles contained in this book, to be completely effective, require regular attendance at church service.

The author takes pleasure in inviting you, should you ever be in New York, to worship in the Marble Collegiate Church, Fifth Avenue and 29th Street, of which he is the minister. He would like you to feel, when in that great city, that you have a church home where you will receive a sincere welcome.

Contents

Part One: THOUGHT CONDITIONERS

Part Two: SELF-IMPROVEMENT HANDBOOK

Part Three: WHAT'S YOUR TROUBLE?

Part Four: SPIRIT LIFTERS

INSPIRING MESSAGES
FOR DAILY LIVING

PART ONE

Thought Conditioners

CHANGE your thoughts and you can change anything. The world in which you live is not determined by outward circumstances nearly so much as by the thoughts which habitually occupy your mind. Even as air conditioners keep the atmosphere of a room fresh and healthful, so THOUGHT CONDITIONERS will give clarity and power to your thoughts, peace to your mind, health to your body and vitality to your life. Since happiness and effectiveness depend upon the kind of thoughts we think, it is absolutely impossible to be happy if we think unhappiness-producing thoughts. One of the wisest men who ever lived was Marcus Aurelius, who said, "A man's life is what his thoughts make of it."

If you put into your mind thoughts of fear, you will get thoughts of fear out of your mind. Fill your mind with resentment thoughts and resentment attitudes will emerge. And in neither case, of course, can you find happiness-inducing thoughts. Whatever the condition of your mind, the THOUGHT CONDITIONERS which I am going to suggest are so powerful that they will displace unhealthy thoughts. Indeed, displacement is the only way you can drive a thought from the mind.

In my experience through a good many years in working with people, I have discovered that the most vital, creative and positive thoughts are those stated in the Bible. Its words are alive. The Bible itself states what its spiritual words will do. "If ye abide in me, and my words abide in you, ye shall ask what ye will, and it shall be done unto you."

3

This means simply that if you fill your mind with spiritual words so that they sink from your conscious to your unconscious mind by a process of spiritual osmosis, you will so condition your personality with spiritual power and sensitivity that God's will can operate in you, and every great value of this life, the ones that really matter, shall be yours. The words of the Bible are powerful THOUGHT CONDITIONERS. They are capable of revolutionising the entire personality.

Method for Using Thought Conditioners

Over the years I had noticed that certain passages from the Scriptures had particularly potent effects on human beings. I began, therefore, to list the life-creating words from the Scriptures which had done me the most good. Many of these I had recommended to others. Some of them had been called to my attention by people in whom there had occurred the most astonishing demonstration of new life and joy. When I applied them to myself I found they did indeed possess tremendous effectiveness.

The process which I have used both personally and in counselling, which has accomplished most impressive results, is simply that of committing these great passages to memory. One puts them in the mind as in a sort of spiritual medicine cabinet, each to be drawn out as needed for specific ills or maladies of the personality, or to meet life's situations as they develop.

As suggested above, the method is also to conceive of these thoughts as having displacement value, crowding out injurious thought patterns.

The best results are gained by utilising spare minutes to

say these scripture passages or THOUGHT CONDITIONERS over and over. As you are riding on a bus or train, or washing the dishes, or waiting for an appointment, utilise fractional moments to dwell and meditate upon the meaning of these texts. As you do so, there will flash out from them new insights, new perceptions of truth. Gradually, by a deep therapy, they will drive into the mind, until presently your life will become a living demonstration of God's power.

Part One contains forty creative and vital passages. Why forty? Primarily because in His own deepest spiritual experience Jesus spent forty days. There is no magic in the number forty, but it so happened that when I finished my list it totalled forty. There are many more vital passages. In fact, you can read and commit the Bible for a lifetime and never exhaust it.

This is my forty, and when you complete these and feel that they are your permanent possession, I suggest that you explore the Scriptures further and find the many others that will have the same health-giving effect in your life.

Now, the method of using this part of this book:

1. I suggest that you read it through quickly at one reading to get the all-over impact of forty of the greatest gems of thought ever spoken.

2. Start at the beginning and memorise one verse a day. Meditate upon the brief message given with each. Definitely practise the simple techniques suggested.

3. It may be that one or two or more of these will have a particularly strong effect upon you. In that case I suggest that you copy it, put it in your pocket, under the glass of your desk or on your dressing-table, so that you can see it every day and thus it can become your dominating thought.

They are not arranged according to problems or categories or days. Neither are they selected on any basis of relative importance. I have listed them just as they have come out of my own mind, one after the other. Perhaps God sorted them for this particular purpose. I give them to you with the prayer that these brief spiritual THOUGHT CONDITIONERS may add to the happiness and usefulness of your life.

This section contains forty health-producing, life-changing, power-creating

Thought Conditioners

Peace I leave with you, my peace I give unto you: not as the world giveth, give I unto you. Let not your heart be troubled, neither let it be afraid. John 14:27

Without a deep inner state of quietness, one becomes prey to tension, worry and ill health. A song, a sunset, moonlight, the sea washing on a sandy shore, these administer a healing balm. But they lack power to penetrate the inner recesses of the soul.

A profound depth therapy is required to attain healing quietness. An habitual repetition of this one text will, in time, permeate your personality with a complete sense of peace.

When tense or restless sit quietly and allow these words to pass unhindered through your thoughts. Conceive of them as spreading a healing balm throughout your mind.

11

The things which are impossible with men are possible with God. Luke 18:27

This text shows how to do an "impossible" thing. Size up your problem, pray about it, do all you can about it. If it seems impossible, don't give up, but affirm, "The things which are impossible with men are possible with God."

Keep relaxed. Don't worry. Avoid getting panicky. Never think, "This can't be done." Declare, "It can be done, it is being done because God is doing it through me." Affirm that the process is in operation. The final outcome may not be entirely what you now desire. But, handled in this manner, the solution will be what God wants it to be.

Renew a right spirit within me. Psalm 51:10

Here is a fragment of a verse which will bring you friends, health, happiness and success. It can improve your disposition.

The word disposition refers to the manner in which you are disposed to react to situations and people. If your automatic emotional reaction is irritable, crabby, selfish, haughty, it impairs or even destroys your relationships.

The quality of your disposition depends upon your inner spirit. This thought conditioner, by the use of the word "renew", implies that when you were created you had a good disposition.

If you have allowed it to deteriorate, Almighty God, who created you, can recreate and renew in you the fine balance, the controlled spirit. He can restore that vital factor in a good disposition, inner quiet control. Let no day pass after today that you do not say many times, "Renew a right spirit within me."

12

Come unto Me, all ye that labour and are heavy laden, and I will give you rest. Matthew 11:28

Perhaps the strain and burden of life have made you tired. If so, maybe you are carrying life too heavily.

Primarily we do not get tired in our muscles, but in our mind. We develop that "I'm swamped" feeling.

Allow this text to dissolve in your thoughts as a kind of spiritual lozenge. As you turn to Jesus in your thoughts, He will give you rest. And how does He do that? One way is by showing you how to work.

"Learn of Me," He says. In other words, work by My method. "My yoke is easy, and My burden is light." That is to say, easy does it. Don't strain, don't tug, relax. Do one job at a time, using the light touch, the easy stroke.

What things soever ye desire, when ye pray, believe that ye receive them, and ye shall have them. Mark 11:24

To pray successfully you must employ affirmation and visualisation. Form a picture in your mind, not of lack or denial or frustration or illness, but of prosperity, abundance, attainment, health. Always remember you will receive as a result of prayer exactly what you think, not what you say. If you pray for achievement but think defeat, your words are idle because your heart has already accepted defeat.

Therefore practise believing that even as you pray you are receiving God's boundless blessings, and they will come to you.

13

Trust in the Lord with all thine heart; and lean not unto thine own understanding. Proverbs 3:5

This text will help you avoid a nervous breakdown. It will stimulate your recovery if you have had one.

A famous neurologist, specialist in nervous breakdowns, often "prescribes" this text for his patients. He writes the words on a card and instructs his patient to commit them to memory and repeat them until they are indelibly printed on the subconscious mind.

The cause of much nervous trouble is frustration. And the antidote to frustration is a calm faith, not in your own cleverness, or in hard toil, but in God's guidance. The cure of frustration is the belief that God will help you obtain your heart's desire. Trust in God with all your heart, and you will be able to keep on working in health and happiness for long years to come.

I am come that they might have life, and that they might have it more abundantly. John 10:10

Many people are lacking in energy. Their vitality is low. They are filled with inner conflicts which dissipate energy. They are dull and apathetic.

What is the secret of energised life? Christ is the answer. It is said of Him, "In Him was life." Fill your mind with Christ, fill your heart with Him, and inevitably energy, vitality, exuberance. delight and eagerness will well up within you.

Every day as you repeat this text make it read: Christ has come that I (fill in your own name) might have life and might have it more abundantly.

14

Confess your faults one to another, and pray one for another, that ye may be healed. The effectual fervent prayer of a righteous man availeth much. James 5:16

God does heal. He does it in two ways, through science and through faith.

In healing, confession is important, for much illness results from buried resentments and guilt. Confession to a competent counsellor releases these poisons, cleanses the mind and soul, thus stopping the passing on of diseased thoughts to the body. Effectual prayer, that is scientific prayer, is very powerful.

The essence of the technique is confess your faults, pray with kindred spirits even if separated by distance, and enthusiastically (fervently) believe.

If God be for us, who can be against us? Romans 8:31

Imagine yourself as actually looking at all your difficulties like an army lined up against you.

Then realise you have a backing that can overcome them all. As you face these enemies of yours—discouragement, frustration, disappointment, hostility, weakness—ask yourself, "What shall I say to these things?" And the answer is, "If God be for us, who can be against us?"

Now spend a minute realising that God is for you and say this affirmation, "God is with me. God is for me. God is greater than all these things."

Then visualise these enemies of your peace and happiness as retreating, giving way before God's power.

Personalise the text by saying: "If God be for *me*, who can be against *me*?"

The repetitive use of this text will give you an enormous sense of God's presence and a powerful feeling of victory.

15

The kingdom of God is within you. Luke 17:21

When you are filled with self-doubt and in the grip of your inferiority complex, don't give up, saying, "I can't do it, I haven't it in me." You *do* have a very big "it" within you. You have the Kingdom of God within you.

God has placed in your personality all the ability you need. You have only to believe in yourself, and strength within you will be released.

In saying the text try it this way, "God's abundance, peace and power are within me. I lack for nothing."

For God hath not given us the spirit of fear; but of power, and of love, and of a sound mind. II Timothy 1:7

Your fears can be healed by this text. It tell us first that fear is overcome by power. What power? There is only one force more powerful than fear, and that is faith. When fear comes to your mind counter it with an affirmation of faith.

Second, love overcomes fear. By love is meant trust, confidence, complete dependence upon God. Practise this attitude and fear will diminish.

The third element is to attain a sound mind in which there are no complexes, quirks and obsessions. Live with the thought of God and you will develop a sound mind where no shadowy fear can lurk.

Whenever you are afraid, verbalise against the thing that you fear, using the words of this text.

16

Thou shalt guide me with thy counsel, and afterward receive me to glory. Psalm 73:24

Perhaps today you have a problem which has baffled you. Try allowing this text to penetrate your mind until it becomes a dominating conception, and it will do some important things for you.

It will make you understand that there *is* an answer to every problem and that God is thinking along with you. It will bring to bear upon your problem that keen and sharp perception of wisdom called insight.

If you put every problem in God's hands, ask Him to give you the right answer, believe that He *is* doing just that, and will take the guidance that comes, your decisions will turn out right.

Wherefore take unto you the whole armour of God, that ye may be able to withstand in the evil day, and having done all, to stand. Ephesians 6:13

This is one of the greatest of all techniques of mental health. It teaches that when we have done all that we can do about a given matter, we are not to get worried or in a panic or be filled with anxiety, but take a calm, philosophical attitude concerning it.

When you have done all that you can do, don't try to do any more, just "stand". Relax, stop, be quiet, don't fuss about it; you have done everything possible; leave the results to God.

God is our refuge and strength, a very present help in trouble.
Psalm 46:1

When trouble strikes, what you want is comfort and protection. You want strength to stand up to it and meet it.

You can have both. This text contains the answer. Frequently remind yourself that God is with you, that He will never fail you, that you can count upon Him. Say these words, "God is with me, helping me."

This will give you a sense of comfort. New hope will flood your mind. New ideas will come. A new sense of power will be felt. As a result you will rise above your trouble.

When a particular trouble arises, before you do anything else about it, sit down quietly, repeat this text a half-dozen times, and put your full faith in it.

He that handleth a matter wisely shall find good: and whoso trusteth in the Lord, happy is he.
Proverbs 16:20

To live successfully one must overcome blundering ineptness, the tendency to do and say the wrong thing. One must develop the deft and skilful touch that makes things turn out right.

A thing does not go wrong because of some perverse fate. It is more than likely that you lack the right slant, the proper approach.

If such is the case, what you need is wisdom. If you let today's text seep from your conscious to your unconscious mind, it will correct the error pattern within you and gradually endow you with wisdom.

Incline your ear, and come unto Me: hear, and your soul shall live.   Isaiah 55:3

Most people live on the surface. They miss the most astonishing things. They see and yet they do not see. And the reason is they aren't really looking.

The same is true about what they hear. They listen with the outer ear only. For example, people go to church, and the Gospel never penetrates beyond the outer consciousness. That is because people do not listen with *all* their faculties. They do not lose themselves in it.

But when a man inclines his ear and hears, listening as though his life depended upon it, getting every word, letting it sink into his mind by a deep and powerful penetration, then the message falls like a healing potency upon him. Every spiritual disease germ is killed, and he lives with new health and strength.

Now unto him that is able to do exceeding abundantly above all that we ask or think, according to the power that worketh in us.   Ephesians 3:20

Today remind yourself that nothing is too good to be true. Your great hopes *can* be realised. Your most wonderful dreams *can* come true. All that you really need you *can* have. An incredible goodness is operating in your behalf.

If you are living a paltry life, resolve to stop it today. Expect great things to happen. Confidently receive God's abundant blessings. Do not think *lack*. Instead, think prosperity, abundance, the best of everything. God wants to give to you, His child, every good thing. Don't hinder His generosity.

Ask, and it shall be given you; seek, and ye shall find; knock, and it shall be opened unto you.   Matthew 7:7

This is a very practical technique of prayer. It works amazingly. One reason we do not get answers to our prayers is that we ask, but do not really expect to receive. We are expert askers, but inexpert receivers.

This spiritual formula tells us to ask and then immediately conceive of ourselves as receiving. For example, to be free from fear, ask the Lord to free you. Then believe that He has immediately done so. The minute you express your faith by sincerely asking Him for a blessing, and believe your prayer is answered, your prayer *is* answered.

I have learned, in whatsoever state I am, therewith to be content.   Philippians 4:11

Your present situation may not be to your liking. Perhaps you are dissatisfied and discouraged. Put the matter in God's hands. If He wants you elsewhere, He will lead you there, providing you are amenable to His will.

But perhaps He wants you where you are. In that case He will help you to adjust to the situation. He will make you content, even grateful for present opportunities. Learn the great art of doing the best you can, with what you have, where you are.

When you do this, you learn how to reach the better condition or how to make your present situation a better one.

My soul, wait thou only upon God; for my expectation is from Him. Psalm 62:5

One of the most serious and powerful facts in human nature is that you are likely to get what you are basically expecting. Spend years developing the mental attitude of expecting that things are not going to turn out well, and you are likely to get that result. You create a mental condition slanted to an unhappy outcome.

If on the contrary you develop and maintain a mental attitude of faith and expectancy, hoping, dreaming, believing, praying, working, you will create conditions in which every good thing can and will grow. Fill your mind with the positive power of spiritual expectancy, and God and His good will flow toward you.

Be ye transformed by the renewing of your mind. Romans 12:2

People often manufacture their own unhappiness by the negative manner in which they think about things. Work with your mind, exercise disciplinary control, and re-slant your thoughts for happier living.

Drain the mind by consciously conceiving of yourself as dropping out every destructive thought, every fear, every inferiority feeling. Picture your mind as completely empty. Then start filling it with thoughts of God, and of Christ, thoughts about every good and pleasant thing. Practise this new habit regularly twice every day, morning and evening, to counteract the older and negative habit of allowing unhappy things to occupy your mind. In due course, unhappy thoughts will not feel at home in your mind, and happy thoughts will transform you.

Be strong and of a good courage; be not afraid, neither be thou dismayed: for the Lord thy God is with thee whithersoever thou goest.   Joshua 1:9

Here is a mental stimulus of tremendous power, which, if received and retained in your consciousness, will give you courage to overcome every difficulty. Nothing can ever dismay you. You may question whether mere words can accomplish so great a result, but never minimise the creative force of an active idea. A mental concept has more voltage than electricity; civilisations are changed by ideas. Emerson said, "Beware of an idea whose time has come."

But as many as received Him, to them gave He power.
                                                        John 1:12

You can possess within yourself all the power you will ever need in life.

The method for securing power is very simple and depends entirely upon you. This text gives the formula. It is to "receive" Christ. When this is sincerely done you will in turn receive power.

And how do you receive Him? Simply decide that you want Him, tell Him so and mean it. Then, starting today, begin to live on a basis you know He would approve.

The essence of the formula is surrender to God's will and Christ's way. It is the acceptance of a new manner of thought and life. Continue to re-surrender yourself every day, and in proportion as you do so you will feel spiritual power surging in.

The thing which I greatly feared is come upon me, and that which I was afraid of is come unto me. Job 3:25

This thought conditioner states a very serious warning. If over a long period of time a person habitually fears something, there is a tendency for that fear to become a reality.

For example, if you fear that you are going to fail, and you constantly entertain thoughts of failure, you will create a mental condition that is conducive to failure. Creative, positive, success factors are repelled by your mind because your mind is filled with defeat attitudes.

On the contrary, if you hold the faith thought, the positive thought, you will create about yourself an atmosphere propitious to success, health and well-being.

This one thing I do, forgetting those things which are behind, and reaching forth unto those things which are before,

I press toward the mark for the prize of the high calling of God in Christ Jesus. Philippians 3:13, 14

Every person, if he is to have mental health and live successfully, must move away from past failures and mistakes and go forward without letting them be a weight upon him.

The art of forgetting is absolutely necessary. Every night when you lie down to sleep practise dropping the day into the past. It is over, finished. Look confidently to the future with God.

23

In all these things we are more than conquerors through Him that loved us.

For I am persuaded, that neither death, nor life, nor angels, nor principalities, nor powers, nor things present, nor things to come,

Nor height, nor depth, nor any other creature, shall be able to separate us from the love of God, which is in Christ Jesus our Lord. Romans 8:37–39

These words mean that no matter what happens, nothing can separate you from God's love and protection. The secret is to build up in your mind day by day the knowledge and realisation of God's presence and His love for you. Dwell on this mentally until it becomes an unshakable fact.

If any man thirst, let him come unto Me, and drink. John 7:37

Every now and then deep unsatisfied longings well up within us. We may seem to have everything the heart can desire and ought to be perfectly satisfied. But still these vague dissatisfactions alloy our happiness.

When you notice such feelings, try saying this verse a few times. As you do so, try to imagine how Jesus looked when He said these words, the kindness, the understanding, the peace on His face. Try picturing yourself as receiving from Him a drink of cold water—symbolic of the water of life that completely satisfies thirst so that one never thirsts again. Affirm that you receive from Him the ultimate in soul satisfaction. A deep inner peace will gradually grow upon you.

Love your enemies, bless them that curse you, do good to them that hate you, and pray for them which despitefully use you, and persecute you.   Matthew 5:44

Make a list of all the people who have hurt and mistreated you or whom you do not like. Then pray for each by name and sincerely practise forgiving each one. Ask the Lord to bless them. Tell the Lord that you want to mean this. Repel the thought that after all you "are justified" in your resentment.

Then speak kindly about these persons to others. Go out of your way to help them. This will in time break down many barriers, but even if it shouldn't, the effect upon you will be amazing. It will clear the channel through which spiritual power flows into you.

I can do all things through Christ which strengtheneth me.
                                        Philippians 4:13

This is an antidote for every defeat feeling. If you feel downed by situations and the going is hard, this statement will remind you that you do not need to depend upon your own strength entirely, but that Christ is with you and is *now* giving you all the help you need.

Teach yourself to believe that through Christ's help you *can* do all things. As you continue this affirmation you will actually experience Christ's help. You will find yourself meeting problems with new mental force. You will carry heavy burdens with ease. Your new "lifting" power will amaze you.

In Him we live, and move, and have our being.

Acts 17:28

This text is a formula for maintaining physical, mental and spiritual energy. The tension and pressure of modern living draw wearily upon our energies. But here we have a renewal method. The text reminds us that God created us and that He can constantly and automatically recreate us. The secret is to maintain contact with God. This channels vitality and energy and constant replenishment into our being.

Every day, preferably about mid-afternoon, when an energy lag usually comes, try repeating this test while visualising yourself as "plugged" into the spiritual line. Affirm that God's recreative energy is restoring strength and power to every part of your body, your mind and your soul.

Thou wilt keep him in perfect peace, whose mind is stayed on Thee.

Isaiah 26:3

If your mind is filled with defeat thoughts, fear thoughts, resentment thoughts, you are bound to be in a state of mental unrest, even turmoil, and of course there can be no inner peace.

This passage advises you to practise thinking about God, to keep your mind "stayed" or fixed, not upon your troubles, but upon God.

Keep your mind on God for as many minutes during the day as possible. This may be difficult at first, for you are unused to spiritual concentration. Practice will make it easier.

26

Whosoever shall say unto this mountain, be thou removed, and be thou cast into the sea; and shall not doubt in his heart, but shall believe that those things which he saith shall come to pass; he shall have whatsoever he saith.   Mark 11:23

Almost alone this passage can revolutionise your life and change defeat into victory.

What does it tell you? That your "mountain", that great rock-like obstruction, that tremendous barrier, can be broken down and ousted from your life. You must not doubt "in your heart". Allow no negative thoughts to exist in your subconscious mind.

Pray that your mountainous difficulty shall be removed and as you pray *believe* that it is being done then and now. Don't have the hazy idea that "this mountain" may be removed sometime in the future, but believe that God is removing it for you now.

They that wait upon the Lord shall renew their strength; they shall mount up with wings as eagles; they shall run, and not be weary; and they shall walk, and not faint.   Isaiah 40:31

This beautiful sentence describes the greatest experience that can ever happen to you. It is called spiritual experience. You get it by completely surrendering yourself to God, and experiencing His presence. Then the heavy weights of your life drop away and you are lifted to eagle-like levels of freedom and power.

But no one can permanently live in such exalted emotional heights. Nevertheless the power stays with you, so that you can move through life with a speed and strength you never had before, you can "run and not be weary". Then, even when you get up against day-by-day situations that used to be difficult and monotonous, this power is so great that it keeps you going without depletion of strength. Spiritual experience begins by lifting you to new high levels, then it helps you to keep going with continuous power.

Eye hath not seen, nor ear heard, neither have entered into the heart of man, the things which God hath prepared for them that love Him.   I Corinthians 2:9

Possibly life has become difficult—even dismal. You may not be getting zest or thrill out of living.

The text for today will restore the old delight in life. It tells you that you have never seen, nor heard, nor even imagined all the marvellous, amazingly fascinating things that God will do for those who love Him, trust Him and put His principles into practice.

As you surrender your life to God, every experience of living will grow increasingly more wonderful.

Cast thy burden upon the Lord, and He shall sustain thee: He shall never suffer the righteous to be moved.

                                Psalm 55:22

A human mind can stand only so much weight. One mental burden piled upon another, unless relief is obtained, will in due course reach your breaking point and cause serious difficulty. Fortunately you do not need to carry your burdens without assistance. God will help you carry them.

But how is this done? It is accomplished in the mind. Practise thinking that God is actually with you. Tell Him about your burdens and believe that He relieves and assists you. Form a picture of yourself as shifting your burdens to Him. He is willing to assume them and is perfectly able to do so. But, and this is most important, don't half give them. And don't take them back. Let God handle them. Leave them with Him.

If any man be in Christ, he is a new creature: old things are passed away; behold all things are become new.

II Corinthians 5:17

Never be discouraged about yourself. You may have tried all your life long to rid yourself of your weaknesses, your obsessions, jealousies, sins, inferiorities, without success. Your failure is probably that you have been trying to make yourself over. That is a long, tedious and essentially impossible project.

But it can be done in no time at all by Christ. All you need do is to say to Him simply, "Lord, I do not want to be this way any more," and mean it. He will do for you what you cannot do for yourself—effect a lasting change in you. Ask Him to change you.

This is the refreshing.

Isaiah 28:12

These few words remind us of a spring of cool water because of their renewing quality. The frequent use of today's text has an invigorating effect.

Sometimes after a busy day, or even in the midst of exacting activities, stop and say these words over to yourself and note how they dissipate weariness and refresh the body, mind and spirit.

The best method for using these words is to say them slowly, emphasising their soft, quiet melody. At the same time conceive of peace, rest and renewal as coming to you.

I sought the Lord, and He heard me, and delivered me from all my fears. Psalm 34:4

A cure for fear that will absolutely work is to get close to God in your thoughts. He is the only certain, unchanging factor in the world. He will never let you down nor forget you. If plagued by fear, do what this text says: "Seek the Lord." That may be done by spending fifteen minutes every day just thinking about God. You can split this up into five-minute periods, but never let a day pass without spending fifteen minutes thinking about God.

Each day make the following statement, "I surrender myself and all my problems, my loved ones, my future into the hands of God, and I trust Him."

Three times every day thank God for all His goodness. Soon your life will be filled with God, and emptied of apprehensions.

When ye stand praying, forgive, if ye have ought against any. Mark 11:25

If you are not getting answers to your prayers, check yourself very thoroughly and honestly as to whether you have resentments in your mind.

Spiritual power cannot pass through a personality where resentment exists. Hate is a non-conductor of spiritual energy.

I suggest that every time you pray add this phrase, "Lord, take from my thought all ill-will, grudges, hates, jealousies." Then practise casting these things from your thoughts.

They shall hunger no more, neither thirst any more; neither shall the sun light on them, nor any heat.

For the lamb which is in the midst of the throne shall feed them, and shall lead them unto living fountains of waters: and God shall wipe away all tears from their eyes.

Revelation 7:16, 17

This is one of the most comforting passages in all literature. It teaches that our loved ones are in a place of peace and beauty. They are under the watchful care of God and regularly experience His tenderness. The deep hunger and thirst of their souls have been satisfied. God, like a loving mother, puts His protection over them and with kindly hand wipes away every tear from their eyes. This He has done for your dear ones who have crossed over to the other side.

If you learn to love this passage and meditate upon it, He will wipe away every tear from your eyes also.

PART TWO
Self-Improvement Handbook

Y OU can be a released, happy and effective personality.
There is nothing hit or miss about efficient living. It
follows definite scientific laws. Learn these laws, which are
simple to apply, sincerely practise them, and you will get
definite results.

If you want to be happy—and who doesn't?—there is a
definite way to go about it. There are specific, easily workable techniques for gaining peace of mind, for overcoming
inferiority feelings, for getting along with other people,
and what is probably even more important, for getting along
with yourself.

This self-improvement handbook is not theoretical. It is
entirely practical. It does not limit itself simply to telling
you that you CAN have the greatest blessings of joy, peace
and love, but it outlines explicit formulas for obtaining them.

The way to use this book is to set aside fifteen minutes
every day. If you are so terribly rushed that you cannot get
fifteen minutes, we will compromise on ten. But if you reduce it below ten minutes, you are not serious about yourself. Nobody is so busy that he cannot reserve ten or fifteen
minutes per day for the improvement of his body, mind
and soul.

This quarter hour, if scrupulously followed, will pay enormous dividends. You will be healthier; you will do better
in your job; your home life will be happier; you will live
longer; and you will have the time of your life LIVING while
you live.

There are two ways to use Part Two, which contains

35

eighteen selected techniques for successful living. FIRST, you may follow them in sequence, practising each lesson in turn. SECOND, you may practise the techniques in a particular lesson, selecting the one that best suits your present need.

While we strongly recommend that you do not use this merely as a book of readings, still it may be wise to read it through so as to have a general idea of the plan and basic teachings before beginning to work with each lesson. This is a suggested action book. Work with only one technique at a time until you feel you have made definite progress in mastering it. Best results will be gained by concentrating on that particular problem. It may take you a number of days to master one formula. If necessary, spend several days on one lesson. This process should condition your mind to an automatic reception of creative spiritual and practical ideas.

Each lesson contains truths which have been tested hundreds of times and which WORK when WORKED. The reader is asked first to read the lesson, then to follow each suggestion made. Let me repeat, this is a directed action book. The purpose is to get results, and if you follow directions faithfully you WILL get results. Use this book sincerely for six months, and you will notice within yourself a deep peace, a steady faith and a sparkling happiness that will make life altogether new and different for you. These simple principles can do wonders in your life.

After reading, studying and practising each lesson, the reader is requested to sit quietly in a relaxed attitude and to conceive of these ideas as sinking, by a mental and spiritual penetration, from his conscious into his unconscious mind. Thus, by the twin procedure of thinking and doing, these concepts will begin at once to work in his body, mind and spirit. A change will start almost immediately. The rate of change in the reader's personality will depend entirely upon (1) his faith, (2) his sincere desire, (3) how faithfully he performs these exercises and (4) the extent to which he yields his mind and heart to the great expert in living, Jesus Christ, from whom all of these techniques are taken.

The author's prayers and best wishes are yours.

LESSON 1

Learn to Relax Your Body

START with your body. That is the nearest thing to you. The body houses your mind, and temporarily your soul. Therefore, all deep relaxation starts at the nearest point— namely, your physical being.

To follow this exercise, first read it, then put the book down and follow each suggestion. As you continue to practice, you will not need to consult the printed steps very often.

Presumably you are reading this while sitting in a chair. But do you know how to sit in a chair?

1. Place both feet squarely on the floor, but do it lightly. Do everything light, strain at nothing.

2. Imagine that you weigh four hundred pounds, and that

this enormous weight is resting squarely on the chair. You are not trying to hold it up. You are letting the chair do that.

3. Raise your right arm high above your head. Make it entirely limp. Then let it fall inertly on your right knee. Repeat this three times.

4. Repeat the process with your left arm.

5. Take three deep breaths, exhaling each slowly, completely emptying the lungs.

6. Allow your head to fall forward as though there was no stiffness in your neck, imagining that it would fall off your shoulders unless attached.

7. Practise relaxing the muscles of your face, letting your face go limp. Repeat to yourself, "My face is limp, my face is limp, every muscle is easing itself."

8. Open the eyes and imagine that little weights are attached to your eyelids. Let the weights close your eyelids. Lift them and let them shut three times.

9. Think of Jesus Christ as being by your side, touching with His healing fingers your eyelids, your face, your heart. Hear Him say to your muscle tension, to your nerves, "Peace, be still." Say the words in the same tone as you imagine He would use, slowly, quietly, lovingly.

10. Imagine now that His healing peace passes through every muscle, all tissue, every blood vessel, to the end of every nerve. Conclude by saying, "The healing grace of Jesus Christ is relaxing, renewing and recreating my physical being, my body, the sacred temple of my soul." Sit quietly with this thought for five minutes, Then arise slowly from your chair and walk slowly. Now you have energy and refreshment for the day.

At any time during the day that you have even a moment, repeat as much of this process as you can. In other words, learn to relax wherever you are, remembering always that out of relaxation comes driving power. Easy does it.

We suggest that you repeat this lesson for at least three successive days if you have any nervous tension whatever, before going on to lesson number two.

LESSON 2

Techniques for Relaxing Your Mind

You are learning to relax your body, but even so your mind may be going around in circles. Bodily relaxation will help to slow down your mind. But inasmuch as you are what you think, if your mind is filled with tension thoughts you cannot successfully relax. So let us go to work on your mind. Let us relax it.

1. Sit relaxed in a chair (as previously described).

2. Think of your mind as the surface of a lake on a storm, tossed by waves and in tumult. But now the waves subside, and the surface of the lake is placid and unruffled.

3. Spend two or three minutes thinking of the most beautiful and peaceful scenes you have ever beheld, as for example, a mountain at sunset, or a deep valley filled with the hush of early morning, or a forest at noonday, or

moonlight upon rippling waters. Go back in your memory and re-live these scenes.

4. Repeat, slowly, quietly, bringing out the melody in each, a series of words which express quietness and peace, as for example, (a) tranquillity (say it very deliberately and in a tranquil manner), (b) serenity, (c) quietness. Think of other such words and repeat them.

5. Make a mental list of times in your life when you have been conscious of God's watchful care and recall how, when you were worried and anxious, He brought things out right and took care of you. Then recite this verse from an old hymn, "So long Thy power hath blest me, sure it STILL will lead me on."

6. Now repeat the following words, which have an amazing power to relax and quiet the mind. "Thou wilt keep him in perfect peace whose mind is stayed on Thee." Repeat this three times.

7. At several times during the day, whenever you have a fraction of a moment, repeat that scripture verse, out loud if possible, so that by the end of the day you will have said it many times. Conceive of these words as active vital ingredients permeating your mind, sending into every area of your thinking a healing balm. This is the best medicine known to man for taking the tension out of the mind.

LESSON 3

How to Get Help from the Bible

FOR multitudes of people, the Bible provides supernatural strength. If it hasn't done so for you, perhaps you need a few simple suggestions on how to make use of this greatest of all tools of happy and efficient living.

You need not be a scholar. Just take a few easy steps and this marvellous book will pour out its riches upon you.

1. Pick it up, open it and read it. It will never do you any good standing on a shelf.

2. Buy an attractive Bible with fine binding, good print, a beautiful book, one that you like to hold in your hand. Learn to love the book itself. Use a Bible that has sentimental value, as for example one given you by your mother, father, pastor or Sunday-school teacher.

3. Read through Matthew, Mark, Luke and John—the first four books of the New Testament. Read one chapter a day. Some people like to read in the morning, but personally I suggest reading your daily chapter just before retiring. This will allow you to go to sleep with the healthiest, happiest, most positive thoughts in the world soaking into your thought patterns for the next day.

By reading a chapter a day, you will complete these four books of the Bible in eighty-nine days. Then repeat the process. Read them over again. Most of the great principles of Jesus are found in these books. Master them, and you will have His rare secret of great living. So, just to be sure about it, when you have read them through twice, read them a third time and the total of the three times will take you two hundred and sixty-seven days.

4. On the second reading of Matthew, Mark, Luke and John, underline passages which particularly appeal to you, and on the third reading, memorise one passage every day. In so doing you are making these thoughts a permanent part of your mental equipment, and the more passages you commit, the more completely you will be carrying the Bible around in your mind. Say these words over to yourself in spare minutes. These passages will serve as logs to cling to when sometimes you find yourself adrift and shipwrecked on the sea of life. They will hold you up and literally save your life.

5. We are afflicted by moods. Sometimes we are fearful and worried; at other times we are angry and resentful; sometimes our loved ones are ill and at times we feel very lonely. There is an answer in the Bible to every mood. So, take your Bible in your hand, close your eyes and pray that God will give you just the message you need. Then open the Bible. The first statement you see may not be your answer, for God does not work in a mechanical manner. Continue reading and you will come to what He wants to say to you—you will recognise it when you see it. Incidentally, this will help you to become familiar with the entire Bible. In time, this familiarity will enable you to know where to look for help in specific situations.

6. Here is a wonderful suggestion. Sometime when you

have a whole evening to give to reading, read the entire book of Psalms without stopping. When you finish you will have such an overwhelming sense of the victory of faith over all the troubles of life that you will want to shout for joy. There is nothing like it. Don't miss it! In cases of grief and great disappointment, I have known this practice to revolutionise the entire outlook of people. It gives one the whole panorama of human suffering and spiritual victory in one dose.

7. It is hoped that you will become so interested in the Bible that you will want to know the entire Book as would a spiritual scholar. If so, consult your minister for suggested books to guide you in your study.

❖❖❖❖❖❖❖❖❖❖❖❖❖❖❖❖❖❖❖❖❖❖❖❖❖❖❖❖❖❖❖❖❖❖❖❖

LESSON 4

Learn How to Pray

❖❖❖❖❖❖❖❖❖❖❖❖❖❖❖❖❖❖❖❖❖❖❖❖❖❖❖❖❖❖❖❖❖❖❖❖

IF you expect to solve your personal problems, have peace of mind and release your powers for great living, you must learn the art of prayer. It just won't come without prayer.

The average person has the idea that by prayer is meant getting down on your knees and saying a few perfunctory words. It is much more than that, for prayer is one of the greatest skills in the world. It is a mechanism by which spiritual power flows from God into the daily lives of human beings. It is the throwing of a switch which releases forces and energies, and it is astonishing how prayer illuminates problems, lifts weights, overcomes obstacles, restores health and brings many other astounding results.

As in any skill or science, one must learn step by step the formula for opening the circuit and receiving this power.

1. What should you say when you pray? Just talk to God as a little boy would talk to a father whom he loves and with whom he feels in harmony. Tell the Lord everything that is on your mind and in your heart.

2. I believe you might find it helpful to talk to the Lord in simple everyday speech. He understands English, and it is not necessary to use an exaggerated formal speech. You would not talk to your father that way, and He is your heavenly Father. In public prayer, a sense of decorum must be maintained, and it is perhaps proper to address God more formally. But in personal and private prayer you might, for example, say, "you" to God rather than "thou". This does not diminish respect for Him and serves to make the relationship more natural.

3. Tell God what you want. You might as well be factual —you want something. Tell Him about it. Tell Him you would like to have it IF He thinks it is good for you. But also say, and mean it, that you will leave it to Him to decide, and you will accept His decision as best for you and others involved. If you do this regularly it will bring to you what you ought to have, and thus fulfil your own destiny. It will be possible for God to give you things that you should have —wonderful things. It is really frightening, the marvellous

things we miss, things God wants to give us and cannot, because we insist upon something else, something only a fraction as fine as He wants to give us.

4. Practise praying as many times during the day as possible. For example, when you are driving your car, instead of the aimless thoughts that go through your mind, talk to God as you drive. If you had a companion on the front seat you would talk to him or her, would you not? Then imagine the Lord is there—for He IS, you know—and just talk to Him about everything. If you are standing waiting for a bus, have a little talk with Him. But at night, when you go to bed, I recommend that you get down on your knees by the bed in the old-time manner and pray. However, if this has been your custom, and it has become merely a stereotyped formality, I suggest that you get into bed, relax and then pray.

5. It isn't always necessary to say words when you pray. Spend a minute just thinking about God. Think how good He is, how kindly, and that He is right by your side guiding you and watching over you.

6. Try helping other people by your prayers. Pray for those who are in trouble or are ill. Pray for your loved ones, and this is very important, pray for people you do not like and for those who have not treated you well. This is probably the most beneficial prayer. It will do more for you to pray for those you resent than for those you love. If you doubt this, give it a six months' trial, and see what happens to you and perhaps also to them.

I am convinced that prayer is an emanation of power. If you "shoot" prayers at people you will profoundly affect them. Select some person who is somewhat of a problem to you and shoot prayers at him. Conceive of yourself as enveloping and surrounding him with healthy prayers, goodwill and faith. I have seen the most astounding results that are almost unbelievable.

7. Whatever you do, do not make all your prayers into the form of asking God for something. The prayer of thanksgiving is much more powerful. Make your prayer consist of a listing of all the fine things you possess, or all the wonderful things that have happened to you. Name them over, thank God for them and make that your whole prayer. You will soon find that these prayers of thanksgiving grow longer and longer, for you will increasingly have more and more things for which to thank God.

LESSON 5

How to Keep from Getting Mad

YOU know how drained out and ashamed you feel after being mad. You may try to tell yourself that you "had a right to get mad", and so you "told them". You may seek to justify the fact that "you let them have it" and didn't "mince any words". All the same, in so doing you have spent a lot of nerve-strength and perhaps made a fool of yourself besides. So you sadly declare, "I'll never do it again." But you will unless you learn how NOT to do it again. And how is that?

1. Remember that anger is an emotion, and an emotion is always warm, even hot. Therefore to reduce an emotion, cool it. And how do you cool it? When a person gets angry, the fists tend to clench, the voice rises in stridency, muscles tense, the body becomes rigid. (Psychologically you are poised for fight, adrenalin shoots through the body.) This is the old caveman hang-over in the nervous system. So, deliberately oppose the heat of this emotion with coolness—freeze it out. Deliberately, by an act of will, keep your hand from clenching. Hold your fingers out straight if necessary. Deliberately reduce your tone, bring it down to a whisper. Nobody can argue in a whisper. Slump in a chair, or even lie down if possible. It is very difficult to get mad lying down.

2. Say out loud to yourself, "Don't be a fool. This won't get me anywhere, so skip it." At that moment it may be a bit hard to pray, but try it anyway; at least conjure up a picture of Jesus Christ in your mind and try to think of Him mad just like you are. You can't, and such thoughts will serve to puncture your angry emotions.

3. One of the best techniques for cooling off anger was suggested by Mrs. Grace Oursler, Executive Editor of *Guideposts* magazine. She used to count ten, but happened to notice that the first ten words of the Lord's Prayer worked better. "Our Father who art in Heaven, hallowed be Thy name." Say that ten times, and before you finish, I am sure anger will have lost its power over you.

4. Anger is a great term expressing the accumulated vehemence of a multitude of minor irritations. These irritations, each rather small in itself, having gathered force by reason of the one being added to the other, finally blaze forth in a fury that often leaves us abashed at ourselves. Therefore, make a list of everything that irritates you, no

matter how inconsequential it may be or how silly it is. List it. The idea in doing this is to dry up the tiny rivulets that feed the great river of anger.

5. Take each separate irritation and make it an object of prayer. Get a victory over each one at a time. Instead of trying to destroy all of your anger, which we have pointed out is a consolidated force, snip away by prayer each annoyance that feeds your anger. In so doing you will weaken it to such a point, that presently you will have control over it.

6. Train yourself every time you feel the surge of anger to say, "Is this really worth what it is going to do to me emotionally? I will make a fool of myself. I will lose my friends." In order to get the full effect of this technique, practice saying to yourself a few times every day, "It is never worth it to get worked up or mad about anything."

7. Finally, this wild, undisciplined, primitive urge in you which flames to the surface can be tamed only by allowing a great Master to take control. Therefore, complete this lesson by saying to Jesus Christ, "Even as you can convert a man's morals, so now I ask you to convert my nerves. As you give me the power over the sins of the flesh, so give me power over the sins of the disposition. Bring my temper under your control. Give me Thy healing peace in my nervous system as well as in my soul." If you are beset by temper, repeat the above prayer three times every day. It might be advisable to print it on a card and put it on your desk, or above the kitchen sink, or in your pocket-book.

LESSON 6

Method for Getting Over Hurt Feelings

ARE your feelings easily hurt? Are you able to get over your hurt? These are two very important questions. For the person who gets his feelings hurt and doesn't know how to snap out of it quickly is a problem to his family, his associates, his friends and, last but not least, to himself.

The head of a large manufacturing organisation says that in his experience, more people fail to get ahead because of their inability to control sensitiveness than one would possibly imagine.

What are some simple steps to take in getting over hurt feelings?

1. When a hurt feeling situation arises, get it straightened out as quickly as possible. Don't brood over it for a minute longer than you can help. Do something about it. Do not allow yourself to sulk or indulge in self-pity. Don't mope around with resentful thoughts. The minute your feelings are hurt, do just as you do when you hurt your finger. Immediately apply the cure. Unless you do this the situation can become distorted out of all proportion. So

put some spiritual iodine on the hurt at once by doing something about it.

2. Apply grievance drainage to your mind. That is, open your mind and let the grievance flow out. Go to someone you trust and pour it out to him until not a vestige of it remains within you. Then forget it.

3. Write a letter telling the person just how you feel about it and tell him how he has hurt you. Don't mince any words. Say everything you are thinking. Fold and seal the letter. Then tear it up, and holding the pieces in your hand, pray for the person and forgive him. Then drop the pieces into the waste-basket and say, "With God's help, I skip it."

4. Ask yourself honestly what there is in you that is so sore to the touch of life. Then ask God to put some healing balm on that sore spot until it heals.

5. Honestly analyse whether in this particular hurt feeling situation you are not more at fault than you are willing to admit. Perhaps you are not, but do not let yourself off easy without a good sharp scrutiny of yourself.

6. The final element in the formula is just to start praying for the person who has hurt your feelings until you feel all the malice fading away. Sometimes you may have to pray for quite a while to get that result. A man told me that he tried this method and he kept account of the number of times he needed to pray until the grievance left and peace came. It was sixty-four times. He literally prayed it out of his system. This is positively guaranteed to work.

7. Say to yourself this little prayer: "May the love of Christ fill my heart." Then add this line: "May the love of Christ for —— (then insert the person's name) flood my soul." Pray this, mean this, and you will get this.

LESSON 7
Let's Actually Practise Forgiving

A NEW YORK physician says that seventy per cent of his
patients reveal resentment in their case-histories. "Ill-
will and grudges help to make people sick. Forgiveness," he
says, "will do more toward getting them well than many
pills." Another physician tells of a patient who died of
"grudgitis"—a long-held hatred of another person. So it is
healthy to forgive, to say nothing of it being the right way
to live.

If you are really serious about self-improvement you had
better do a resentment removal job on yourself. What are
some practical steps to take? How shall you proceed to
achieve a forgiving attitude? Carefully and painstakingly do
the following:

1. Determine that you are going to do this even if it
requires great effort to overcome discouragement. It is not
easy to revise deep attitudes. You may be inclined to abandon the effort because it will seem so hard, but hang on.
In due time you will feel the resentment leave you.

Christ recognised the difficulty you may have in learning to forgive for He said to "forgive seventy times seven"

if necessary. To be literal, that means 490 times. I prophesy that long before you have forgiven a person 490 times, you will be free of your resentment.

2. Remember the harm resentment can do, not to the other person, but to you, even to making you ill.

3. Remember that you will never be spiritually blessed until you forgive. This is a basic spiritual law. Goodwill cannot flow toward you unless it flows from you.

4. Thinking about forgiving is not enough. You must come to a specific moment when you say, "with God's help I NOW forgive." (Do that at THIS moment, now, as you read this and be positive.)

5. Repeat the Lord's Prayer, inserting your offender's name, "Forgive ME MY trespasses as I forgive ———."

6. Practise praying for the other person, asking specific blessing for him, especially concerning matters which would previously have annoyed you the most. This will have an amazing curative effect on you and perhaps on the other person. Stop reading and do that NOW. This is a book of action, not a philosophising treatise. Results come from action NOW.

7. Speak in a kindly manner as often as possible about a person against whom you harbour antagonism.

8. Write a brief letter of goodwill. Do not be offended if it is not answered. You have cleansed your own heart; that is what really matters. Write the letter now as you finish this reading.

9. Study the factors which created this unhappy situation to correct the "mistake pattern" in yourself. This will reduce the possibility of similar conflicts in the future.

10. Ask Christ now to effect a permanent spiritual change in your nature to forestall future rifts. Ask for a rebirth with all resentment tendencies removed. Sincerely want

this, pray for it, believe it is given you and you will have it. When you have nothing in your heart against anyone, you will be amazed at the new power and happiness which will be yours.

❖◆❖◆❖◆❖◆❖◆❖◆❖◆❖◆❖◆❖◆❖◆❖◆❖◆❖◆❖◆❖◆❖◆❖

LESSON 8

How to Break Your Worry Habit

❖◆❖◆❖◆❖◆❖◆❖◆❖◆❖◆❖◆❖◆❖◆❖◆❖◆❖◆❖◆❖◆❖◆❖

Y OU do not need to worry. Actually it is only a mental habit taken on from others. You were not born with it, you acquired it. Because you can change any habit and remove any acquired attitude, you CAN cast out worry from your mind. Many people waste half their energy worrying. There is just one time to stop worrying, and that is TODAY. So, practise the following formula and give your personal worries the greatest blow they ever received. Do this well, and they will never recover from it. You can be permanently free from worry by practising the following lesson.

1. Know that worry IS a habit; you have practised worrying for so long it has become a mind set.

2. Fully realise the harm worry can do. It is the most disintegrating enemy of human personality, man's greatest plague. People say, "I'm sick from worry", and then

laughingly add, "not really sick, of course." But they can be, and often are, actually ill from worry.

3. Remind yourself that your worries fall into three percentage categories (according to a study of case histories by a group of physicians who established worry as the greatest cause of illness), 40 per cent of your worries are about the past; 50 per cent about the future; 10 per cent about present matters.

4. To be rid of worries about past mistakes, practise the art of forgetting—NEVER LOOK BACK. Every morning upon arising and every evening at retiring, repeat one of the greatest aids to mental health. "Forgetting those things which are behind and reaching forth unto those things which are before, I press forward." Repeat that NOW three times, slowly.

5. Meditate on a wise statement by William James, the great psychologist: "The essence of genius is to know WHAT to overlook." Say that quotation out loud and commit it to memory.

6. Affirm faith in your future—and in the world's future. Remind yourself that despite all the troubles and difficulties that are with us, someone else is also with us; namely, God. He has been here a long time and is not likely to depart from you or any of us who trust Him.

7. Practise the art of imperturbability. Whatever the stress, affirm, "God is keeping me calm and peaceful." Worry rolls off the imperturbable mind like water off a duck's back.

8. Now practise emptying the mind, saying, "I am NOW emptying my mind of all anxiety, fear, insecurity." Imaginatively do this NOW. Think of yourself as reaching into your mind and one by one removing the worries. A child has an imaginative skill beyond that of adults. A hurt can

be kissed away or thrown out of the window. It works for him because he believes that is the end of it, and so it proves to be. Jesus says for you to become "as a little child".

9. Practise filling the mind. Say, "God is NOW filling my mind with peace—with courage—with calm assurance."

10. Practise God's presence, saying, "God is with me NOW. God is my constant companion. God will never leave me." The practice of the presence of God, the companionship of Christ is a certain shield against worry. Would you worry if He were ACTUALLY with you? There is no IF about it. He said He would be, and so He is.

❖❖❖

LESSON 9

Learn to Make Your Work Easy

❖❖❖

NOBODY does good work who tugs and strains and is rigid about it. "Easy does it" is the proper method.

The person who works the easiest, does the most in the shortest time and his work shows the mark of skill. Don't live and work the hard way. So we suggest that you study and master the following rules for making your work easy.

1. Drop the idea that you are Atlas carrying the world on

your shoulders. The world would go on even without YOU. Don't take yourself so seriously.

2. Tell yourself that you like your work. It may be difficult to make yourself believe that, for you may have talked yourself into hating it. Or you may be a "fighter of the job", that is to say, you struggle against it rather than with it. This emphasis on liking your job will tend to make it a pleasure instead of a drudgery. Perhaps you do not need to change your job. Change yourself and your work will seem different.

3. Plan your work for today and every day, then work your plan. Lack of system produces that "I'm swamped" feeling. To arrange work in an orderly way and perform it in the same manner makes the total job infinitely easier.

4. Decide that you will not try to do everything at once. That is why time is spread out. Repeat the wise advice from the Bible, "This ONE thing I do." Say that to yourself NOW, three times, emphasising the word ONE. One step at a time will get you there much more surely than haphazardly leaping and jumping. It is the steady pace, the consistent speed that leads most efficiently from start to destination.

5. Practise becoming expert in correct mental attitudes, remembering that ease or difficulty in your work depends upon HOW you think about it. Think it is hard, and it is hard. Think it is easy, and it is easy. So spend a minute now in the practice of thinking of your work as easy.

6. Determine now to re-study your job, for "knowledge is power" (over your job). It is always easier to do a thing right. Make your own job analysis to discover more right ways of doing things. The right way is right, because it meets less resistance and is therefore easier than the wrong way.

7. Practise being relaxed about your work. Again remind

yourself that "Easy always does it." Do not press or strain. Take your work in your stride. One way to do this is to repeat such a work formula as the following: "I can handle this job. I know this material or this business. I am well informed about it and am competent to deal with it, therefore I will have no fear or nervousness about it and, besides, God is with me to help me." This will give you a feeling of peace and confidence and you can do the job in a relaxed frame of mind.

8. Discipline yourself not to put off until tomorrow what you can do today. Accumulations make the job harder than it actually is or should be. Do not drag yesterday's burdens along with you. Keep your work up to schedule. Spend a minute NOW listing the things to do today, and tomorrow, and the next day. This will immediately relieve today's burden, for usually you do not need to do so much right now, as you nervously think you do. If your mind gets the idea that you have too much to do, it immediately accepts tired thoughts, your energy drops and the job becomes heavy and hard.

9. Pray about your work, today's work. You will get some of your best ideas that way. Never start a day or any job without praying about it.

10. Take on the "unseen partner". It is surprising the load He will take off you. God is as much at home in offices, factories, shops, as in churches. Do not spurn God's help, for He has broad shoulders and strong arms and wonderful ideas. All are available to you. He knows more about your business than you do. His help will make your work easy.

LESSON 10

Method for Making Important Decisions

IT is said that history turns on small hinges. So does a human career result from an accumulating series of decisions about large and small matters over a period of years. But the catch is, that you can never know when a seemingly small decision may prove to be, from the prospect of later years, the big decision of your life.

Following are some simple steps which are designed to help you make right decisions.

1. Get quiet. You are going to need all your faculties. Only a quiet mind can think at maximum efficiency. So get into a quiet place, sit down and compose yourself. Practise the technique of relaxation in Lesson 1. Pass a few quiet thoughts through your mind. Read again Lesson 2, on Relaxation of the Mind.

2. Repeat three times the following text from Psalm 72:24: "Thou shalt guide me with thy counsel and afterward receive me to glory." In this confused, bewildering and inscrutable world in which none of us has the wit and wisdom to see very far or clearly, we have access to God's advice and counsel. That is to say, God will advise us in

making decisions. How can you go wrong if you take His advice? Therefore, in any decision you are about to make, affirm that you are receiving God's advice.

3. Now, deliberately conceive of God's advice as passing into your mind and that in due time you will "know" what that advice is. Obviously you will hear no voice nor see any writing, but by process of spiritual telepathy—the inner voice—God will transmit the right idea to you. It will come over the network of spiritual illumination. If you must have that advice today, you will get it. If you do not need it until next week, let us say Monday at eleven o'clock, you will have it then, if you believe that you will, and if you keep calm and continue to pray and think.

4. Consciously allow Jesus Christ to condition your mind to correct thinking. Say over to yourself three times the following words from Philippians 2:5: "Let this mind be in you, which was also in Christ Jesus." It has been said "we can nestle into Plato's brain and think from there". That means that we can get up into the vast brain of Plato and see things as he saw them. But colossal as was Plato's brain, there is an even greater brain, into the heights of which we can climb and see with clarity and breadth of knowledge far above ourselves. Imagine therefore that you are considering your problem in the great brain of Christ.

5. Ask yourself the simple question, "What would Jesus do in this decision?" What He would do would be the right thing, would it not? Right now, ask God to take all wrong and error out of your heart. Remember that right can never come out wrong. To get right answers, YOU have to be right.

6. Do not hurry your decision. Weigh your problem carefully. Allow it to soak in the mind, or to change the figure, let it simmer. Never force a decision. If you properly

condition the mind the decision will emerge when completely done.

7. Take just a moment to thank God for giving you the right answer, for He is giving it to you, and thank Him for the great happiness which is in your heart, knowing that you are so spiritually right that the element of error has been profoundly lessened. You are going to get the RIGHT answer.

8. Do you know when you have the right answer? Mr. J. L. Kraft, eminent food manufacturer, says, "I pray hard and think hard, and when the time is up and I must have the answer, and I have done all the praying and thinking I can do, I just say, 'Lord, please show me the next thing to do.' Then," says Mr. Kraft, "I believe that the first idea that comes into my mind is the answer. And," he added, "I have been correct a large enough percentage of times to convince me that this process is sound."

9. Having received your answer, trust it wholeheartedly. Do not accept it with doubt. Do not look back and hash it all over again. Take it with faith and thanksgiving. If you have sought God's counsel and prayed earnestly, your answer will come up as a clear, bright light burning in the mind. You can trust it to lead you through all darkness. God will see you through.

LESSON 11

Make an Inventory of Your Joys

To improve yourself, do not discount the importance of cultivating joy. Some athletic coaches train the beginner in tennis, golf and other sports, by directing him to sing as he plays. It has the effect of unlocking the muscles and producing that fine correlation of eye, nerve and muscle which is necessary in executing an efficient stroke or shot.

Great players who have an inwardly happy disposition are more released and do not make the errors that come to the tied-up personality. "Red" Barber, the sports announcer, says that disposition is a factor of basic importance in a star baseball player.

To release yourself for your job, to get all your powers correlated and flowing toward your objective rather than away from it, begin to practise inner joy. You will be surprised at how many joys you have. The old hymn offers wise advice, "Count your blessings, name them one by one."

Most unhappy people are very inexpert in blessing-counting, but they can total their troubles and worries with the speed of an adding machine. That is because they have practised trouble-adding for so long that they do it by second nature.

How do you practise inner joy?

1. Make an inventory of your joys.

Get a blank piece of paper and a pencil. Head the paper, My Joys and Blessings. Start with:

(a) I am thankful that I am strong enough to sit up and push this pencil across the paper.

(b) I am thankful that I live in a country where freedom still endures.

(c) I am thankful that I have a good water-tight roof over my head, enough to eat and enough to wear.

2. Continue to make your own list, omitting nothing because it is small or commonplace—you would miss these so-called commonplaces if you did not have them.

3. Make a list of all the things in your daily experience which should fill you with happiness, such as your home, where there is a good dinner awaiting you, the dear faces of your family around the table, a comfortable chair, a lamp, an open fireplace. Complete your own list and repeat it over to yourself every day.

4. Step outside the house after you finish this lesson and take five deep breaths of good fresh air. Note every beautiful thing around you and think about it, such as the moonlight on the lawn and its silvery radiance falling against an old church steeple, or making the house across the way stand out in white loveliness against the night. Consider the pattern of the sunlight falling through the trees on to a well-kept green lawn. Take pleasure in a lighted train rushing through the night, or the quiet stars twinkling in the sky, or the sound of the crunch of snow under your foot on a winter's night. Get your mind on these things, which are

the essence of life. Relish them and they will make your heart sing within you.

5. Do an unexpected favour for someone and note the look of happy surprise in his eyes. This will fill you with joy.

6. Overcome something: a fear, a jealousy, a grudge or a temptation. The glow of happiness and satisfaction which follows will make you realise that real delight in life does not consist of giving in, but in getting over.

7. Sing at least one song every day. This may not add to the enjoyment of your family or friends, but it will be a wonderful tonic for you, and the songs that can put the most happiness into your heart are religious songs. If you do not already know them, learn a few of the great old hymns and sing one every day. A hymn with the morning bath is a fine idea, as it will wash you on the inside just as soap and water do on the outside.

8. Compose your soul every night by doing two things. Ask the Lord to forgive you for any wrong done, or ill-will, and thank Him for His goodness. A quiet joy will steal through your whole soul and you will sleep like a baby while happiness becomes your second nature.

LESSON 12

How to Make Your Personality Attractive

PERHAPS this is particularly interesting to the ladies. When they get ready to go to a meeting or a party, or even shopping, they powder and fuss to add to the attractiveness of their physical beings.

Both men and women will get further and do better by making their personalities more attractive. A personality "do" is fully as important as a "hair-do". Personality "cosmetics" will put charm and colour into the drabbest personality and the most colourless countenance.

Men will find that a physical setting-up exercise will not set them up half so much as some simple spiritual conditioning.

Here are a few steps to take in making your personality attractive.

1. Let a series of happy thoughts run through your mind. They will show on your face.

2. Spend a minute or two forgetting your pet grudges and peeves. Just bring up each one in your mind, then say, "Forget it."

3. Practise letting peaceful expressions rest for a minute

on your face—it will help to stand before the mirror while doing this.

4. Hold yourself erect, head high, stomach in, chest out, and think a series of positive thoughts; meanwhile expel every negative idea.

5. Spend a minute definitely thinking thoughts of kindliness. Remember all the kind acts that have been done for you lately or that you have observed.

6. Say to yourself slowly, "Let the beauty of the Lord my God be upon me," and conceive of God's attractiveness as being conferred upon you.

7. Select a few people to be particularly kind to today, those you were a little harsh with yesterday. Perhaps they are close to you: husband, wife, children—the bus driver.

8. Go out today with the thought that an inner light is shining out of you. People will notice and comment, "What an attractive personality." But do not take undue pride in this; for if you do, the light will fade. Just be natural, and the light will glow with a never-failing radiance.

LESSON 13

Formula for Overcoming Your Inferiority Complex

WE could not begin to tell you how many ask the question "How can I rid myself of my inferiority complex?" Perhaps nothing so plagues and harasses human beings as the crippling, misery-producing feeling of personal inadequacy. You can be cured of this trouble though you have probably suffered from it since childhood.

You do not need to shrink before anybody or anything, and in the next fifteen minutes you can start the process which will lead to the end of your inferiority feelings.

1. Stamp indelibly on your mind a mental picture of yourself succeeding. Your mind will seek to develop this picture. Never think of yourself as failing. That is most dangerous, for the mind always tries to complete what it pictures. So ALWAYS picture "success".

2. Whenever a negative thought about yourself comes to mind, deliberately voice a positive thought to cancel it out.

3. Do not build up obstacles in your imagination. Depreciate every so-called obstacle. Minimise them. Difficulties must be studied to be eliminated, but they must be seen for

only what they are and must not be inflated by fear thoughts.

4. Do not be awestruck by other people and try to copy them. Nobody can be you as efficiently as YOU can. Remember also that most people, despite their confident appearance and demeanour, are as scared of things as you are.

5. Repeat ten times a day these words: "If God be FOR me, who can be AGAINST me." (Repeat them NOW slowly and confidently.)

6. Get a competent counsellor to help you understand why you do what you do. Learn the origin of your inferiority feelings, which often begin in childhood. Self-knowledge leads to a cure.

7. Ten times each day practise the following affirmation, repeating it out loud if possible: "I can do all things through Christ who giveth me the strength." Repeat those words NOW. These words constitute the most powerful antidote on earth to inferiority thoughts.

8. Make a true estimate of your own ability, then raise it 10 per cent. Do not become egotistical, but develop a wholesome self-respect. Do that NOW.

9. Put yourself in God's hands and believe you are NOW receiving all the power you need.

10. Remind yourself that God is with you and nothing can defeat you. He said, "Ye shall receive power after the Holy Spirit is come upon you." So yield yourself to the Holy Spirit by saying, "I want the Holy Spirit in my heart—I now receive it." Then believe that God will make good His promise and believe further that you now RECEIVE the power He promises and gives.

LESSON 14

What to Do When a Loved One Is Ill

WHEN a loved one is taken ill and you are deeply concerned, what can you do to help that is of a practical spiritual nature?

1. Follow the advice of a prominent medical school head who said, "In sickness, send for your minister, even as you send for your doctor." In other words, believe that spiritual force as well as medical technique are important in healing.

2. Pray for the doctor. Realise that God uses trained human instrumentality to aid His healing powers. As one doctor has put it, "We treat the patient and God heals him." Pray therefore that the doctor may be an open channel of God's healing grace.

3. Whatever you do, do not become panicky or filled with fear, for if you do, you will send out negative and therefore destructive thoughts in the direction of your loved one when he requires positive and healing thoughts to assist him.

4. Remember that God does nothing except by law. Also remember that our little materialistic laws are only fragmentary revelations of the great power flowing through

the universe. Spiritual law also governs sickness. God has arranged two remedies for all sickness. One is healing through natural laws applicable by science, and the other brings healing by spiritual law applicable through faith.

5. Completely surrender your loved one into the hands of God. By your faith you can place him in the flow of Divine power. There is healing there, but in order for it to be effective, the patient must be completely released to the operation of God's will. This is difficult to understand and equally difficult to perform, but it is a fact that if the great desire for the loved one to live is matched with an equally great willingness to relinquish him to God, healing powers are amazingly set in motion.

6. It is also important that harmony prevail in the family; that is, a spiritual harmony. Remember the emphasis in the scripture, St. Matthew 18:19, "If two of you shall AGREE on earth as touching anything that they shall ask, it shall be done for them of my Father which is in heaven." Apparently disharmony and disease are akin.

7. Form a picture in your mind of the loved one as being well. Visualise him in perfect health. Picture him as radiant with the love and goodness of God. The conscious mind may suggest sickness, even death, but nine-tenths of your mind is in the subconscious. Let the picture of health sink into the subconscious and this powerful part of your mind will send forth radiant health energy. What we believe in the subconscious we usually get. Unless your faith controls the subconscious, you will never get any good thing, for the subconscious gives back only what your real thought is. If the real thought is negative, the results will also be negative. If the real thought is positive, you will get positive and healing results.

8. Be perfectly natural. Ask God to heal your loved one.

That is what you want with all your heart, so ask Him please to do it, but we suggest you say PLEASE just once. Thereafter in your prayer, thank Him for His goodness. This will help to release deep spiritual joy through reassurance of God's presence and His loving care. This joy will sustain you, and remember that joy itself possesses healing power.

LESSON 15

Overcome Your Negative Attitudes

Oₙₑ of the basic facts of human experience is that usually you get what your mental attitude indicates. That is, if you believe you can, you can. If you believe you cannot, you cannot. Think negatively, and you will get a negative result because by your thoughts you create a negative atmosphere which is hospitable to negative reactions. On the contrary, think positively, and you create a positive atmosphere which makes positive results a certainty.

A close-up of one of the most successful men in America, who started with almost less than nothing, reveals that one of his most outstanding characteristics is that he never even so much as entertains the THOUGHT of failure in any undertaking.

How does one go about shifting from a negative to a positive thought pattern?

1. For the next twenty-four hours deliberately speak hopefully about everything: about your job, about your children's marks in school, about your health and about your future. Speak hopefully about the prospects for world peace and the business outlook and go out of your way to talk optimistically about everything. This will be difficult, for it is your habit to talk pessimistically, and from this habit you must restrain yourself by an act of will.

2. After speaking hopefully for twenty-four hours, continue the practice for one week, then you can be permitted to be "realistic" for a day or two. You will discover that what you meant by "realistic" a week ago, was actually pessimistic, but what you now mean by "realistic" is something entirely different: it is the dawning of optimism. When most people say they are being "realistic" they delude themselves, for they are simply being negative.

3. You must feed your mind even as you feed your body, and to make your mind healthy you must feed it good, nourishing, wholesome thoughts. Therefore, now, today, start to shift your mind to positive thinking. Start at the beginning of the New Testament and underscore every sentence that has to do with FAITH. Continue this until you have marked every such passage in the four books, Matthew, Mark, Luke and John. In Lesson 3 you were asked to memorize passages that appealed to you; now you should emphasise passages dealing with FAITH, but before we start this process, turn to St. Mark, Chapter 11, and commit to memory verses 22, 23 and 24. They will serve as samples of the verses you are to underscore.

4. Then begin to commit the underscored passages to memory. Commit one each day until you can recite the

entire list. This will take time, but remember, you have consumed much more time in becoming a negative thinker than this will take you, and it will require not a little time to unlearn your negative thought patterns.

5. Make a list of your friends and determine who is the most positive thinker among them and deliberately cultivate his society. Do not abandon your negative friends, but get closer to those with a positive point of view for a while, until you have absorbed their spirit, then you can go back among your negative friends and give them your newly acquired thought pattern.

6. Be careful to avoid argument, but whenever a negative attitude is expressed, oppose it with a positive and optimistic opinion.

7. Pray a great deal, and let your prayer take the form of thanksgiving on the assumption that God is giving you great and wonderful things, for if you think He is, He surely will. God cannot give you any greater blessing than you can believe in. He wants to give you great things, but even He cannot make you take anything greater than you are equipped to receive.

Make as your motto this statement: "If ye have faith as a mustard seed . . . nothing shall be impossible unto you."

LESSON 16

Handling Your Disappointments Skilfully

A FAMOUS neurologist who has treated many cases of nervous breakdown says, "Frustration, feelings of futility and disappointment create such a heavy burden on the personality that many people give way under it." Then he adds, "People will be healthier, happier and live more efficiently when they learn how to handle their disappointments skilfully." Let us learn and begin to practise that skill in this lesson.

1. Think of every disappointment as a message from God. He is trying by this means to tell you something. Perhaps He is saying, "No—that is not good for you; no—that is not the way to do it." You are bound to be disappointed if you do not do a thing in the right way. Only God is perfect rightness. If you are going at your problems in the wrong way, things are bound to go wrong, even though it is something you want to do. Therefore, if you suffer disappointment it is wise to assume that the disappointment is a message from God. He is shaking His head and saying, "No—you haven't got it right."

2. Your disappointment may take the form of an unfulfilled

hope, a frustrated ambition, the death of a loved one or the failure of something at which you have worked diligently. It should still be regarded as a message from God, that the outcome is part of a plan which He regards as best, though disappointing to you. You will find peace and comfort and the right direction by acquiescing, without bitterness, to His will.

3. I suggest adopting the practice of a successful business woman who commits every day to God. Before she starts out in the morning, she puts the entire day in God's hands. As a result of this, she says that nothing can be a disappointment, because whatever happens is according to His plan and will. It changes DIS-appointment to HIS appointment. The most wonderful things happen, she declares, as a result of this plan of daily living. Psalm 37:5 describes it thus: "Commit thy way unto the Lord; trust also in Him; and He shall bring it to pass."

4. When you have done all you can about a matter and the result is disappointing, and no further thought or activity can improve the situation, practise leaving it behind. Do not drag the heavy weight of a disappointment along through life with you. Say to yourself, "Well, I have done all I can and I am disappointed—this must be the way God wants it to be, therefore I will accept the situation." One of the greatest texts in the Bible in helping to leave disappointment behind is Philippians 3:13, "Forgetting those things which are behind, and reaching forth unto those things which are before, I press toward the mark of the prize of the high calling of God in Christ Jesus." Even now, as you read this, say to yourself, "I drop this; I leave it; I walk away from it."

5. If there is still something you can do about a matter, do not give in to your disappointment. Keep praying about

it. Keep working at it. Keep believing in it. Thomas A. Edison wanted to make a nickel–iron–alkaline battery. He performed fifty thousand experiments and failed fifty thousand times. Someone asked him, "Aren't all these failures disappointing to you?" "Not at all," replied Mr. Edison, "for I have learned fifty thousand ways it cannot be done and therefore I am fifty thousand times nearer the final successful experiment." Of course that successful experiment came, and he made his battery. Edison was a genius, that is true, but a large part of his genius consisted in never yielding to disappointment and quitting.

6. In the previous point we brought out the fact that Edison utilised his disappointments to advantage, for he allowed each disappointment, by showing him how NOT to do it, to guide him to the way TO DO it. Therefore, keep yourself open to the plan God has for you. If, let us say, you suffer one disappointment after another, it is possible that you are trying to force open doors that God does not want you to enter. Keep working at life prayerfully, then these disappointments or, as in the case of Edison, unsuccessful experiments, will lead you to the right door.

7. Meditate on the meaning of the word disappointment. The prefix DIS denotes separation from. Used in connection with the word appointment, it means separation from your appointment. This implies that there is an appointment for you, but you have missed your appointment, hence there is a DISappointment. The solution is to say to the Lord, quietly and humbly, "Lord, correct the error in me by which I have missed the appointment you have for me, and guide me to it."

❖❖

LESSON 17

How to Get Along with People

❖❖

No self-improvement book should omit one of the most important of all human skills; namely, the ability to get along with people—an art in which many fail. They rub each other the wrong way. They are difficult to handle. They are touchy and uncertain and one can never be sure just how they will react. Such persons are often passed by when the time arrives for advancement, and fail to get the full confidence of others, to say nothing of their affection and esteem.

How may one develop skill in getting along with others?

1. Definitely practise loving people. It is true that this requires effort and continued practice, for some are not very lovable, or so it seems—with emphasis upon "seems". Every person has lovable qualities when you really learn to know him.

2. Practise changing your critical attitude toward your fellow men and get in the habit of looking for something to praise. Once you start picking at people critically, you will find yourself criticising everything they do. Reverse this

mental attitude by finding something, however small, to praise in everyone.

3. If you dislike someone, take a piece of paper and try to make a list of everything you can possibly admire about that person. Try to increase your list on this individual from day to day.

4. Practise believing in people and show them that you believe in them. While it is true that occasionally someone in whom you believe will fail you, in the greater number of cases your belief in a person will awaken in him a corresponding belief in you. There is something in human nature that tried to live up to the opinion people have one for the other. Build up a person in your own mind; that will cause you to like him better and it certainly will make him like you because your esteem of him raises his ego.

5. Practise helping others. Do something every day for as many as you can. Never do it in expectation of something in return. Be aggressively helpful just because it is the kindly and Christian thing to do. It can be guaranteed definitely that, as you develop the attitude of helping others, you will win their affection. This is the surest way of learning how to get along with people.

6. Make a list of the people whom you do not like, or who have irritated or even harmed you. Then go right down the list and pray for each one by name, and forgive them as you pray. Conceive of your prayers as reaching out and surrounding them with love. I have seen such astonishing results of this practice that it would be difficult to convince me that there is not an emanation of power in prayer that definitely affects people. It may require time—even as a block of ice which is thick requires lots of sunshine to melt it—but it melts eventually.

7. Watch for every opportunity to congratulate a person

on his birthday, or about his children, or upon some achievement attained by his efforts. Write him in case of sorrow or disappointment—in other words, look for every chance to say the right word, and always do it sincerely, without any expectation of return.

8. Pray daily that all self-consciousness may leave you and that when with other people you may be your own happy, natural and released self. Then when you are thus released from the inhibitions of self, people will like you because God has made the wholesome, natural individual that you really are to be attractive and likeable.

❖❖❖

LESSON 18

How to Have a Christian Experience

❖❖❖

THOUGH we call this a self-improvement book, a man can no more change himself by himself, than a leopard can change its spots. The real art of self-improvement is Christ improvement. What this book has taught you to do in a series of practical lessons is to SURRENDER your life to control by Jesus Christ. HE effects the change in you. The greatest step forward in self-improvement is through spiritual experience.

It is the same kind of experience as falling in love, only deeper and more profound. Sometimes it is called "spiritual awakening". Something happens deep within you and thereafter you are filled with light and warmth and beauty. This may happen quickly and dramatically. On the other hand, it may be a developing experience unfolding as the rose, beginning with the bud and ending with the full flowering. In either case, you will have that feeling described in the words "Were not our hearts strangely warmed within us?"

This is the greatest experience possible to a human being. Tolstoy described it in an immortal phrase—"To know God is to live." The result is a transformed, changed life, the ultimate in personality improvement.

In addition to all the lessons in this book which you have studied and practised, what final steps shall you take to have this, the most important of all human experiences?

1. Realise that you have already begun the process of spiritual experience if you have faithfully followed the lessons in this book. You have been practising self-improvement and spiritual change because the lessons have been devised as definite spiritual exercises.

2. NOW give up everything in your life that you know in your heart to be wrong. You cannot compromise or rationalise if you want full spiritual power. There is no dodging this issue. You know this is so. We simply remind you that in your self-improvement plan you have arrived at the moment when this separation must be made.

3. Eliminate from your heart forever all hatred, resentment, jealousy and grudges. You must sincerely forgive everyone against whom you hold resentment.

4. In so far as it is humanly possible, make amends for any wrong you have done to other persons. If no amends

are possible, pray that God in His own way will make it right for you, then ask to be forgiven, believe that the matter is cancelled out, and forget it.

5. Realise that in the last analysis you are changed not by any act YOU perform, but through faith in Christ, who alone can make you a new person. As the Scripture puts it, "If any man be in Christ, he is a new creature, old things are passed away, all things are become new." You can greatly help to improve yourself by diligent practice, but the final act of personality improvement is a gift conferred upon you through humble faith in Him.

6. Start to live the new life. This may not be easy at first. Deeply implanted thought patterns and negative thinking habits treated in this book will still try to resume their control over you. Old errors of thinking and doing will endeavour to re-assert themselves like a defective needle playing in the same old groove on a record. But if you simply start living the new life, assuming that you will be successful and KEEP LIVING IT, you WILL be successful. Old habit resistances will give way to the new habit, and this will happen more quickly than you imagine. Simply start living the glorious new life today and believe that with God's help you are going forward to better things. Believe that every day will see you stronger and happier. For a life of inner peace and power, start now and you have such a life—NOW. Believe that God has heard your prayer and granted your request. Accept the fact that you are now a "new creature", a transformed person.

7. To continue to grow in this new life, practise and re-practise the lessons in this book. Also become active in your church and carry this message of the new life to others. Realise that the world can be saved from its failures and unhappiness by a chain reaction of vital new life.

PART THREE
What's Your Trouble?

WHAT'S your trouble is written for the very definite purpose of helping anyone who has a trouble. This part of our book contains fourteen lessons in how to solve everyday situations. The solutions suggested have been tried, for they are the result of years of experience in dealing with the personal problems of hundreds of people who have come to the religio-psychological counselling clinic in the Marble Collegiate Church, Fifth Avenue and 29th Street, New York City. Because so many have been freed from their troubles through the application of certain tested principles, it is believed that these lessons can help you too, if you use them faithfully as outlined.

It is suggested that you read this entire section before beginning to utilise specific lessons dealing with particular problems. This over-all reading will give you a clear idea of the plan and scope, and also the basic methodology which is presented.

The next step is to re-read and then apply, point by point, the lesson that deals with your most pressing problem. The points outlined under each lesson will bring definite results within a short time, depending upon the completeness with which you co-operate and the perseverance which you demonstrate. Accordingly it is suggested that you work with one problem for several days before undertaking another.

In similar fashion use each lesson which bears upon your needs.

These lessons are also designed for discussion group purposes. They can very well be used as discussion material for a series of fourteen weeks. The problems with which they deal will be found in any group.

Some of the points outlined in the lessons may require considerable analysis and study to derive their full meaning and usefulness. Hence, group or family discussion is important.

After you have worked with a lesson for a few days, score yourself on the basis of how completely you have applied each point in the lesson.

As the author of these lessons, I want to assure you of my absolute belief in the workability of the principles outlined. I *know* you can derive great benefit from the sincere application of the steps suggested here because of the amazing results attained by so many who have applied this system of thought and action. Of course, these procedures are based on the practical teachings of Jesus Christ. May the Lord help you to enter into a life that is more wonderful than anything you have ever known.

I Am a Worrier

1. You have stated the basis of your trouble when you say, "I am a worrier," for that means you have made it a habit. Primarily, worry is just that, a very bad mental habit. And you can change any habit.

2. You became a worrier by practising worry. You can become free of worry by practising the opposite and stronger habit of faith. With all the strength and perseverance you can command, start practising faith.

3. How do you practise faith? First thing every morning before you arise say out loud three times, "I believe, I believe, I believe."

4. Pray, using this formula, "I place this day, my life, my loved ones, my work in the Lord's hands. There is no harm in the Lord's hands, only good. Whatever happens, whatever results, if I am in the Lord's hands it is the Lord's will and it is good."

5. Practise saying something positive concerning everything about which you have been talking negatively. Talk positively. For example, don't say, "This is going to be a terrible day." Instead affirm, "This is going to be a glorious

day." Don't say, "I'll never be able to do that." Instead affirm, "With God's help I will do that."

6. Never participate in a worry conversation. Shoot an injection of faith into all your conversations. A group of people talking pessimistically can infect every person in the group with negativism. But by talking things up rather than down you can drive off that atmosphere and make everyone feel hopeful and happy.

7. One reason you are a worrier is that your mind is literally saturated with apprehension thoughts, defeat thoughts, gloomy thoughts. To counteract, mark every passage in the Bible that speaks of faith, hope, happiness, glory, radiance. Commit each to memory. Say them over and over again until these creative thoughts saturate your subconscious mind. Then the subconscious will return to you what you have given it; namely optimism, not worry.

8. Cultivate friendships with hopeful people. Surround yourself with friends who think positive, faith-producing thoughts and who send out that atmosphere. This will keep you re-stimulated with faith attitudes.

9. See how many people you can help cure of their own worry habit. In helping another to overcome worry you get greater power over it within yourself.

10. Every day of your life conceive of yourself as living in partnership and companionship with Jesus Christ. If He actually walked by your side, would you be worried or afraid? Well, then, say to yourself, "He is with me." Affirm aloud, "I am with you always." Then change it to say, "He is with me *now*." Repeat that affirmation three times every day.

After Happy Years We Are Drifting Apart

1. THE start of the healing of a breach between husband and wife is to recognise, as you have done, that the old comradeship has been impaired. A frank facing of that fact is primary. Then determine, with God's help, to do something about it at once. Any marriage that has years of happiness back of it can be saved by intelligent and spiritual solutions.

2. Together, if both parties will work in such co-operation, make an analytical study of your lives to determine where and for what reason the drift apart began. In other words, go back to the crossroads. It is important to discover the cause or causes of the widening breach. Many of these so-called "causes", upon mature analysis, will seem of no value. Others that do create a real issue may be successfully resolved by intelligent discussion and prayer.

3. Let each partner carefully consider his own failures and acknowledge them to the other. Do not stress the other's derelictions. Try to accept more blame than the other person, and the other partner will not want to be

outdone in accepting his share of responsibility. Mutual forgiveness often quickly follows this procedure.

4. If there is another man or woman in the picture, face that problem without hysteria and ask God's help in devising a spiritual strategy by which you can win back your partner. And remember, you have the advantage because your own love dates from youth, you have worked together over the years, you have the ties of children, your relationship is legal and respectable, while the other is clandestine and unrespectable. There is a basic affinity between your partner and yourself. Explore the reasons why you are no longer attractive to the other. Go to work to restore the original attraction, for it can be done. Believe that God is helping you and that you cannot fail.

5. Marriage to the very end of life must never be taken for granted. Always seek to keep the element of romance alive. Do not become prosaic, dowdy, careless, unattractive personally. Do not be unattentive, unappreciative. Be a good housekeeper, a good provider. Be gallant, be feminine. As the health cycles of life proceed in each partner, as grey hairs appear, enter into these changing conditions with understanding, tenderness and the realisation that each period of life has its own rich reward. Remind yourself that God planned it that way, and those who follow God's plan receive marvellous blessings.

6. Make an analysis of your respective interests. If the survey shows that you are interested in widely varying things, you have one important explanation for the cleavage. These apparently harmless differences in likes and dislikes may have caused you to drift apart without suspecting what was taking place. Decide on some common interests; as many as possible. Let each partner develop as much liking as he can for the other's interests. Eliminate any interests

of your own which you are aware take you away from the other. Do as many things as possible together.

7. The greatest of all techniques in healing a marriage breach is to pray together. Kneel down side by side and let each one pray. The voice in prayer has a much different tone than in argument. Immediately the couple is lifted to a higher level and a third party enters the discussion, and in that atmosphere bickering fades away. Life's most beautiful values are re-emphasised. The old pure love tends to return and the guidance of God enters into the minds of both.

8. Go to church together. This enables you to rise to high levels of spiritual experience together and it puts the touch of sacredness upon your relationship. It is a fact that church-going families stay together. Statistics show that a large percentage of those who drift apart have allowed prayer, Bible reading, church-going to disappear from their lives.

I Have Been Warned I Must Slow Up—or Else

1. THIS is a sensible warning and is not without a mixture
of blessing. The person who heeds such a warning and
conserves his nervous energy will live longer and do a better
job in life. This caution is not a notice of doom but is
rather an assurance of longer and healthier life if one learns
to live sensibly.

2. Embrace this situation as an opportunity to take stock
of the time values of life. Why have you been driving yourself and living in such a state of tension? What is this
feverish activity all about? I am sure you will come up with
the answer that now is the time to pray earnestly about
your life. In so doing you will learn God's way to live,
which is with peace and quietness, and therefore with greater
power than you have ever known before.

3. This warning to slow up will probably reveal that you
are not completely in harmony or in tune with the recreative
power of God. You have lost connection with the flow of
energy and life renewal, hence this impending crack-up.
Reattach your life, by means of prayer and self-surrender,
to the Divine recreative energy and health, and you will

experience a resurgence of strength, first of soul, then in mind and finally in the body. Unbroken contact with God provides automatic life renewal and is an important factor in overcoming heart attacks and kindred maladies.

4. Fix in your mind this absolute truth that you are not going to be a lame duck. You will get as much, if not more, accomplished at the reduced pace at which you must now live as you did formerly by your hectic and nervous tension. Easy does it is the proper technique, for easy really does it. You have tried to carry the world on your shoulders. Now shift the heaviest part of the weight to God's shoulders. Do this by imaginatively conceiving of yourself as actually letting go as God takes hold. This will give you a new power and perspective in your job, because now you will be master of the job rather than be mastered by it.

5. Adopt the most effective of all health combinations, God and your doctor. Follow your doctor's advice carefully, and with equal fidelity apply the healing techniques of the Great Physician. Copy from your New Testament every passage that deals with peace, quietness, renewal. As for example this statement, "And the whole multitude sought to touch Him: for there went virtue out of Him, and healed them all." Commit such passages to memory and affirm your belief that Jesus Christ heals nowadays just as He did in Bible times. Affirm that He is healing you now. Picture Christ making you well.

6. Every morning, every night and three times in between engage in the following practice. Believe that the hand of Jesus Christ with its healing touch is laid upon your head and every affected part. Relax your body, close your eyes and imagine the feel of His touch. Conceive of a healing power as passing into your being. Affirm the following. Say it out loud if possible. If not, repeat it quietly,

"Jesus Christ is touching me. The healing Grace of Christ is making me well. I yield myself to Him. I am receiving His healing." Then give thanks and surrender yourself to Christ.

7. Oftentimes the stress that culminates in heart trouble and hypertension is not primarily a result of overwork. It frequently arises from a more fundamental cause; namely guilt. Sins committed and unforgiven cause deep anxiety and apprehension. The unconscious feeling that one should be punished causes him to chastise himself by hard work and extra effort as a compensatory mechanism. Guilt often creates hecticness. If you have a sense of guilt, talk it out with a wise counsellor, get it forgiven; and in due course your feverish tempo will subside.

8. Perhaps your warning came in order that you may have a deeper experience of God in your life. You, perhaps, have been too busy to know God or to permit Him to do anything with you. Now He slows you down in order that He may fill you with His Grace, His peace and satisfaction. Therefore, accept your warning as a means for finally attaining that inner happiness you have been seeking all your life.

Things Irritate Me

1. IF something is unsatisfactory, take the attitude of doing whatever you can about it. And when you can do nothing further, practise viewing it dispassionately as did St. Paul, "Having done all, stand."

2. Practise adjusting yourself to situations, things, conditions and people on the principle that such are what they are. Change and improve them if you can. If you cannot, then accept the inevitability of your own adjustment to them.

3. In any situation, however annoying, there must be some satisfactory factors. List them and concentrate your thought upon them.

4. Remind yourself that things might be worse. Think for a moment of these worse possibilities as being actual. Then say to yourself, "But the worst factors have not happened," and see if your attitude does not become less irritated, indeed, more thankful.

5. Adopt the philosophy of taking things as they come. This is the way God made the world. Perhaps this law is designed to test our ability to demonstrate imperturbability.

Learn to take things without surprise, without petulance, in the recognition that such is just the way things are.

6. When things go wrong or do not suit you, practise tolerance and a spirit of charity toward those responsible. Give them the benefit of the supposition that they are doing their best, sincerely trying to do all they can about it.

7. When the tendency toward irritation comes on, take three deep breaths in, then out. Relax by lying down if possible (it is hard to be irritated lying down). If not, relax in a chair, letting go the muscle tension. Then recite the Twenty-third Psalm just once. Do it slowly and quietly. Dwell for a moment on the mental picture of the "still waters".

8. Affirm this statement: "The peace of God that passeth understanding is now flooding my mind, my body, my soul." Say this three times, and repeat the process several times during the period of stress, until the tension passes.

9. Accentuate the deliberateness of your actions and of your speech to counteract the impetuous and sharp re-actions which irritation tends to cause. As irritation grips you, try being lackadaisical and lazily indifferent toward the circumstances which stimulated your annoyance.

10. Affirm the following every morning before starting out the day: "The quieting, restraining, healing hand of Jesus Christ is resting upon me now. His presence shall be with me throughout this day and shall help me calmly and with control to meet every situation that shall develop. He takes my irritations away."

I Am Lonely

1. REALISE that lots of other people are lonely too, so look around for those who seem to be alone and show an interest in them. You will be surprised how quickly many such people will come to depend upon you, and this will help to alleviate your own loneliness.

2. Study yourself to discover why you have so few friends. Honestly analyse. Ask what it is that fails to attract other people. Are you dull in conversation, hard to get along with, critical, not neat and attractive in dress, deficient in intellectual interest or other factors? Consult your pastor as a counsellor regarding this problem to be sure your analysis is objective.

3. Study and master the art of being a good conversationalist. Read books, newspapers and form opinions, but don't present them as though you know it all. Do not get argumentative, but have something thoughtful to say about matters that interest people. Get some sparkle into your conversation. Don't be a clam.

4. Learn how to tell a happy story. Make a list of such stories and be alert in conversation to recognise the place

where such stories would add a unique touch. When you tell a story put your whole self into it. Then let the other fellow tell one. Give him genuine interest and appreciation. In other words, participate but don't monopolise. Always try to bring the other person out rather than bring attention to yourself. Others will like you for this if you do it genuinely.

5. Develop a prayer list. Every day pray for those on your list. Send out thoughts of prayerful interest toward them. Whether you ever become close to these people or not, by praying for them you are sharing your deepest personality with them, and thus they are your friends. It is amazing how many times your circle is enlarged by this procedure.

6. Look for opportunities to bring encouragement, especially to those who suffer sickness, sorrow, disappointment. Telephone or write or call upon them and offer Christian support and friendliness. Also, join in people's successes and joys by sending a word of congratulation or pleasure in the happiness that has come to them. The idea is to lose in other people's lives that self-centredness which is basic in your present loneliness.

7. Practise developing a great mental storehouse of pleasant and happy thoughts, memories, ideas, experiences. When alone, draw them one by one into the centre of consciousness and live them over, or meditate upon their rich meaning. The person who does this effectively is never at a loss for good company, for he is his own good company.

8. Live with Christ in your mind. Would you be lonely if you could actually spend a day with Christ? It would be the one supreme day of your life on earth. You can do this, for He is with us always. Talk with Him aloud if possible. Imagine He sits in a chair in your room or walks

beside you. Talk to Him just as you would to a friend. The more you do this the more real He will become. Moreover, this spiritual friendship will do something to you that will draw others to you. Christ in you will irresistibly attract people to you, for you will have something for them and they will recognise that fact.

9. It is all as simple as going around doing good in Christ's name. But don't act pious. Be normal and genuine, happy and self-forgetting, as Jesus was and is.

10. It is also as simple as the old adage, "To have friends, be friendly." But to be truly friendly one must learn the magnificent art of friendliness by association with the greatest Friend of all. Whoever learns friendship from Him gains and keeps the affection and devotion of others. Such a person will no longer be lonely.

I Am So Tense

1. YOUR trouble indicates that you are tied up, taut, drawn up tight like a rubber band. But understand this fact: the tautness is probably not in your actual nerves or in your physical body. It is in your mind. The tense thoughts

in your mind make your body feel tense because the nerves obey the thoughts.

2. A cure is to fill the mind with habitual peace thoughts rather than mental attitudes of tension.

3. Practise daily the process of draining or emptying the mind of thoughts that make you tense. Do this by using the following affirmation: "I now empty my mind of all irritation, all frustration, all hate, all worry, all impurity." As you do this, visualise a stream of impurities flowing out of your mind.

4. Follow the above by a second affirmation: "I am now filling my mind with peace, with love, with purity, with calmness, with faith." As you do this, form a mental picture of a pure stream of thought flowing down a channel into your mind, cleaning and refreshing it. Perform points three and four in this lesson at least twice every day.

5. Practise systematic exercises of relaxation to reduce muscle tensions derived from thought tension. (Such exercises are outlined rather fully in our SELF-IMPROVEMENT HANDBOOK, Part Two, Lessons 1 and 2.) One simple method for relaxation is to stop occasionally and take three deep breaths. As you exhale say, "I am breathing out tension thoughts." As you deeply inhale affirm, "I am breathing in peace thoughts."

6. Sit in an easy-chair, place your feet squarely on the floor. Let your head fall back against the head-rest, imagine that little lead weights are on your eyelids. Open your eyes and conceive of the lead weights as pulling your eyelids shut. Let the muscles of your face relax by thinking some quiet thoughts. Notice how your face feels rested.

7. Practise imaginative visualisation by bringing into your mind pictures of peaceful scenes. Examples are, a full moon shining down upon a snow-covered earth; or a quiet

stream flowing through a beautiful meadow on a sunlit summer afternoon. Practise holding such pictures in your mind for a minute or two when you feel tense.

8. Make a list of peaceful and quieting words and periodically say them over to yourself. Repeat these words slowly, expressing their full melody. Make the saying of them as musical as possible and meditate upon each word. Suggested words are: tranquillity, serenity, imperturbability.

9. Honestly face and eradicate any guilt feelings or sinfulness, for it is out of these poison-pockets that tension often develops. There can be no peace of mind unless there is also peace of soul.

10. Eliminate, by the process of forgiveness, any ill-will, hatred, resentment and jealousy. These are evil mischief-makers that keep you stirred up and in a turmoil in the essence of your nature. When you truly forgive, they will be driven off and, like a healing balm, peacefulness will come into your mind and pass through your entire being—physical as well as emotional.

11. Underline in your Bible all passages expressing the peace of God. Commit these to memory and often say them over. As you do so, conceive of their healing quietness as touching your entire personality with that ineffable peace which is the true cure for tenseness.

We Are Worried About Money

1. REMIND yourself that you will never correct this situation by remaining in a state of worry. You need to think creatively, and it is impossible to develop creative thoughts out of a mind that is agitated. Therefore, ask God to give you a peaceful mind through which He can send an answer to your problem.

2. Remind yourself that God will supply all your needs out of His vast abundance. If only a little trickle has been coming through to you from God's storehouse of prosperity, it may be that something in you or your situation prevents the supply ducts from being fully opened.

3. Ask yourself if you are thinking "lack". There is a curious law that if you think lack you tend to create a condition of lack. Shift your thought pattern to one of abundance and believe that God is now in the process of giving you the abundance you need. Repel all lack thoughts, practise abundance thoughts. In ways that will amaze you, your needs will begin to be satisfied.

4. Look through all inspirational literature you can find for the life-stories of people in like situations who have

utilised some simple idea to improve their financial condition. Do not dismiss such stories on the false argument that you could not have a similar experience or that there was something unique about these people. They are no different from yourself. They, too, despaired. But they found a solution to money problems. So can you. The best such creative inspirational literature is the monthly magazine *Guideposts*, Pawling, New York.

5. Seek to have complete family co-operation on expenses. Make yours a family budget to be family spent. That is, Mary had a pair of shoes last month, so John gets a new shirt this month, Bill a pair of slacks next month. Plan and pray over your expenditures as a family, and each member will feel pride and co-operation as the budget is controlled and spent on the basis of a new efficiency.

6. Practise the good old American principle of thrift and frugality. This requires spiritual power, for it involves self-discipline. It is perhaps not easy, but it is good for us to deny ourselves. Pray and ask God, "Do I really need this?" The pleasure of working and planning and saving for something adds delight to life, and besides it has a beneficial effect on the budget. Prayerised control of spending brings both financial and spiritual blessings.

7. Take all your bills; lay them out on the table. Then ask God what to do about them. Ask Him for a definite plan of financing. Then systematise your expenses, your debts and your income. Make a plan of payment, economy, saving and spending on the basis of the insight you receive through your prayers. Most financial problems can be solved through system, especially a God-guided plan of systematic management.

8. Are you giving a tithe to God's work? A tithe means a tenth. That may seem a good deal. We would not advocate

it if we did not believe that the giving of a tithe sets in motion forces which will bring God's abundance toward you. Meditate upon God's promise: "Bring ye all the tithes into the storehouse . . . and prove me now herewith, saith the Lord of hosts, if I will not open you the windows of heaven, and pour you out a blessing, that there shall not be room enough to receive it."

❖❖

Resentment Is My Problem

❖❖

1. You are right, resentment can be a real problem. It not only makes you unhappy, but it can also make you ill. Physicians' tests indicate that resentment is often a pronounced factor in illness. As one doctor said, "He could be a well man if he got hate out of his heart."

2. The first step in eliminating resentment is to stop deluding yourself that your resentment is justified. Perhaps you have plenty of reason to be hurt, but resentment is never justified. In the last analysis resentment will do you more damage if you keep it up than any hurt you are now experiencing.

3. Work with yourself until you truly and with all your heart want to let go of your resentment. Sometimes the sadistic element in human nature nurses a resentment with secret unhappy pleasure, even as you bite down on a painful tooth. Want mental health so completely that you also want to be rid of your resentment.

4. Be honest with yourself. Ask yourself if your resentment is caused by a feeling of guilt for your own failures, which you have refused to admit and are rationalising, thus blaming other people, through an active resentment, for your own deficiencies.

5. Pray it out. Just start praying and keep at it until you feel the resentment pass away. One man told me that he had to pray 167 prayers before his resentment was dissolved. But it passed, never to return. Perhaps this is why the Bible says, "Pray without ceasing." The process is a simple one. The heart and soul are so filled with prayers that there is no room left for resentment. Your prayers channel in the Grace of Jesus Christ which makes you clean inwardly.

6. One of the first prayers to offer is for the Grace to pray for the person against whom your resentment is directed. This is important, for at the beginning of this process you may feel it hypocritical to pray for him or her. But if you pray for the Grace to do so, you will be lifted to a new level of spiritual understanding and strength. On this higher level you have more greatness than before, and then you can pray with sincerity.

7. Definitely, wholeheartedly, humbly and sincerely pray, mentioning the name of the one you resent. But do not simply ask that you may forgive him. Pray for positive blessings to come to him. Send out a spiritual wish that he may experience a fullness and richness of life. Be very

careful not to pray for his improvement, for in so doing you may merely be criticising him under the guise of holiness.

8. Start thinking kindly thoughts about this person and look for opportunities to express kindly sentiments concerning him.

9. Give him an opportunity to do you a favour. There is a curious law in human nature that we tend to like persons for whom we render a service, provided sincere appreciation is shown and a desire to reciprocate. I heard of two neighbours who were hostile. Something went wrong with the furnace of one. Grudgingly he called upon his belligerent neighbour for assistance, for the latter was a furnace expert. This gave the neighbour an opportunity to show his ability, and at the same time to feel the other's dependence. The first man was an excellent gardener. As summer came, vegetables repaid the kindness. Friendship followed.

10. Develop the habit of looking for people's good points. Everybody has them.

There Is an Alcoholic in Our Family

1. Do not regard this as a disgrace. Your loved one is ill, for alcoholism is a disease. It yields to both medical and spiritual treatment, especially the latter. This is not to minimise the spiritual defeat of the liquor habit.

2. The alcoholic can be cured. Therefore assume an attitude of faith that your loved one will, by the Grace of God, conquer this malady. You may be sure of this, for the reason that thousands of alcoholics have overcome their defeat and are now useful and successful members of society.

3. Immediately contact Alcoholics Anonymous. This is one of the greatest and most effective groups of helpful people. They have reclaimed over one quarter of a million alcoholics. They will take your alcoholic under their personal care and will not give up until he or she is restored.

4. It is important to know that part of the cure, and a definite requirement in A.A., is that a person who is an alcoholic shall admit it. He must sincerely take the attitude that he has no strength within himself to combat this disease and is willing to follow the programme and especially yield to a higher power; namely, God.

5. Be prepared for the difficult fact that often an alcoholic must sink to the depths before his mind will accept the fact that he cannot handle even one drink of liquor. He may have to be thrown to the earth by his habit before he will admit that it has complete power over him, as abhorrent as that fact may be. When he arrives at this sad state, hope begins. For now, admitting that he has no power, he is ready to accept the Grace of God through which he shall receive power.

6. Inasmuch as you are dealing with an irrational individual temporarily out of control, the victim of an appetite which he cannot manage, all members of his family must be prepared for all manner of embarrassment and disappointment. You must practise a long-suffering attitude. Even when he starts to improve he may slip back. His loved ones must never be discouraged, but exercise boundless faith even when it seems hopeless. Pray for him, love him, hold unremitting faith that the miracle of his rebirth will take place.

7. Pray for patience and you will receive it, and you will need it, for sometimes the process is protracted. It would be a pity if, at just about the time the victory was near, you would give up. Remember the words of the Scriptures, "In your patience possess ye your souls." In such patience you will also win sobriety for your loved one. Believe that God will heal your loved one if you will hold on, if you will have faith. Continually help Him with your prayers.

8. Remember that the surest way never to become an alcoholic is never to drink. It is liquor that makes alcoholics, and nothing else.

9. Take your alcoholic to church every time the church door is open if possible. Subject him to every spiritual atmosphere available. Get him active in the church. Ask your

minister to take him on and give him spiritual friendship and guidance. Surround him with prayer, and, to use the great old word that has amazing power in it, seek to get him converted. Conversion can change an alcoholic. I have seen it happen countless times. As the A.A.'s often say, "There but for the Grace of God go I . . ." With all your heart and with all the faith you can muster, put your alcoholic in the hands of God. Ask God to heal him and believe that He will. According to your faith shall it be done unto you.

10. For a detailed process of helping an alcoholic, one that has proved successful in many cases, read Chapter Nine of my book, A GUIDE TO CONFIDENT LIVING.*

I Find It Difficult to Adjust to Retirement

1. WHY use the word "retirement"? Think of it as a change from one pattern of life to another. The fact that you are making this change, perhaps after many years, makes it no less a shift from one form of activity to another. The concept "retirement" suggests that one is through. He retires or leaves the active scene. He abandons participation. Life "readjustment" is a better concept.

* Published by The World's Work.

2. Ask God through prayer to guide you to some constructive activity which will keep you busily occupied, yet perhaps not under the demanding strain to which you have been accustomed. Consecrate to God's disposal your years of experience on the basis of your present strength and energy.

3. Whatever you do, repulse with all your spiritual and personality force the idea that your constructive life is ended. Entertain the thought that some of the greatest contributions of your life can be made in these latter years. You have all the required assets, experience, maturity, understanding. And God will supply you with new eagerness, hope and faith.

4. Gather together people of your own age in your community, many of whom may not possess your resourcefulness. Form a "Golden Years Club" or a "Late Sixty Club" or an "Early Seventy Club" or a "Three Score and Ten Society". Do not sit around and wait for young people to entertain you. By all means do not rely upon your children. Keep independent of them. Give such organisations a spiritual as well as social meaning.

5. Do not emphasise in your conversations or in your thoughts how old you are. Remember that the time measurement called a year is entirely artificial. Time is measureless. You are no older than you will admit yourself to be. So live that people will never think of age when they are with you. Be an ageless type of person. Keep your mind alert, your faith in God strong, and time will deal easily with you.

6. Look around your community for some job that needs to be done in the church, in community service, in politics or in helpfulness to some businessman. Do not sit and pine. Get out and work at one thing after another that captivates your interest until you find the activity best suited to you.

There are plenty of things that need to be done in any community. Don't wait to be asked. Just go and do them. One retired man I know is the chief spark plug of the Chamber of Commerce in his town, where they haven't enough money to hire a general secretary. He went to the office one day and said he would do anything. They asked him to receive callers. He did it so well that he made many new friends for the Chamber. Now they cannot get along without him.

7. Get the idea firmly fixed in your mind that no man is through until God calls him home. God is the one to decide when you are through. As long as He leaves you here He has work for you to do.

8. Get a lot of fun out of life: fish, tour, walk, play golf, enjoy yourself, and have no feeling of guilt in doing it. And do all you can, with God's help, to make other people happy.

9. Pray for God's guidance. Tell the Lord that you have finished one job. You may have worked at it for a long time. Now you are free for the next job He wants you to do. Believe there is such a job. Be alert to recognise it when it appears and believe that you are going to have the time of your life doing this new and zestful thing.

A Loved One Has Died

1. THE important first step in meeting your sorrow is to ask Jesus Christ to assuage your anguish and believe that He does so. The greatest of all antidotes to sorrow is to believe that Christ administers His healing balm to your wounded heart. This process is accomplished through most earnest and continuous prayer. Under the circumstances it may be hard for you to pray. But just pour it all out to Him as a child who is hurt would cry out to an earthly parent.

2. Do not hesitate to give free expression to your grief. Plainly speaking, cry about it. This is one of nature's release mechanisms. Attempting to suppress your sorrow, on the false assumption that an expression of grief is not the part of a cultivated person, is to run the danger of developing a psychosis. Nature established within us a process of naturalness. If you thwart this you do yourself an injury. Your grief must flow out, else it will congeal within you and in that event there can be no relief.

3. Practise being a philosophical person, saying: "Everyone must have his share of grief; this is the way it is with humanity's life. I have had my loved one and no one can

take my memories from me. Besides, I still have my dear one in my heart. I must stand up to life no matter how many blows it gives me. God will see me through." Talk to yourself that way until your mind accepts this courageously philosophical attitude and you find yourself living on that basis. While this is not easy, it will serve to comfort you. And it is a fact that when you affirm strength and courage you develop them.

4. Keep on living in the same old way as far as possible. Do not avoid people and places to which you were previously jointly accustomed. Carry on in your interests, activities, associations as before. To run away and hide yourself is a procedure that tends to develop into chronic moroseness and in extreme cases makes of one a hermit or abnormal introvert. Immersing yourself in the main stream of living helps to soften the pain of sorrow by drawing a large proportion of your thought energy away from your sorrow and applying it to other matters, and it is in the thoughts that the pain is felt. I assure you there is no disloyalty to your departed loved one by this attitude. On the contrary, it may be that your loved one, watching from heaven, may be distressed by your withdrawal, for in his now deeper wisdom he may understand the sad consequences to you of such an attitude. Get back into life. Christ will sustain you.

5. There is a strange law of life to the effect that by taking upon yourself an additional weight of sorrow in the form of the heartaches of others, you mitigate and may even lose your own grief. This is explained by the fact that emotional spiritual energies, exhausted in assisting other people, have little power left to produce grief pains for yourself. Therefore, deliberately list persons who have suffered sorrow and give all the time possible to the project of helping them to

alleviate their grief. This is one of the surest methods of eliminating your own heartache.

6. If your sorrow persists, I suggest the following quick remedy. Start at the beginning of the Book of Psalms and read them from beginning to end. The Psalms contain the whole range of human life with its woes and victories, and are filled with such profound faith and understanding that a saturation of your mind by these noble teachings will help you to achieve spiritual understanding and serenity. This is a spiritual-action method of great power.

7. Personally I have found that one of the most certain of all sources of comfort is the conviction that one does not lose a loved one by death. True, the form of his existence is changed, but he is not dead. This we may know by the fact that now and then we get a sense of his or her presence and feel that they overshadow and surround us with their loving tenderness. In addition to this sacred experience is the dear old Christian belief that we shall be reunited with our loved ones in that land where there is no separation. You can believe this. It is absolutely true. "I am the resurrection, and the life: he that believeth in Me, though he were dead, yet shall he live: And whoever liveth and believeth in Me shall never die."

Our Son Is Keeping Company with Someone of Whom We Disapprove

1. A BASIC and primary attitude to take if your son or daughter is keeping company with someone of whom you disapprove is to keep calm about the matter. Do not get excited. Be careful what you say. This is a delicate relationship and your own influence is always enhanced by composure. And then, also, the probabilities are that if you keep your head things will turn out better than you now contemplate.

2. Engage in some very searching prayer. Ask God to make you entirely objective and honest, both in your appraisal of the young man or young woman involved and also as to whether your pride is dictating your attitude rather than what is best for all concerned.

3. Consider the fact that it is very dangerous to attempt to determine the life of another adult person, and young people quickly become adult these days. Their instinct may be sounder than yours in the selection of a mate. If you insist upon your own choice, and in later years that choice proves to be a wrong one, you may get the undying resentment of your child. You may even harm the life of your own son or daughter.

4. If you are proceeding on a calm, sensible, prayerful basis your insight may be sounder than that of your young person, for young people often act impulsively, later to regret such impetuousness. A God-guided parent will know what to say, when to say it and how to express it.

5. Use your originality to get your young people associated with the proper kind of friends. Deliberately seek to bring into their circle the type of high-minded, intelligent young people of character and background of whom you do approve. If as a parent, for example, you do not go to church, I suggest that in the churches nowadays you will find the highest type of young people, intelligent, capable and sophisticated. Associate yourself, therefore, with church families, remembering that propinquity is the forerunner of romance.

6. As a minister, having counselled with parents who were absolutely sure their children were marrying unwisely because they felt that the proposed life-partners came from families that were "beneath them", or did not themselves "measure up", I have been impressed by the large proportion of times in which the disapproved young person became outstanding and the marriage proved happy.

7. The best thing any parent can do as a daily procedure is to put his child, through prayer, in the hands of God and affirm that God will guide him. This process of surrender and affirmation of guidance will actually surround the young person with a spiritually protective force.

8. If you want to influence for good your child's matrimonial experience, parents should endeavour to create a marriage example which will cause their children to want the same kind of marriage relationship as their parents. They will unconsciously seek a husband or a wife according to the standards and type under which they have grown up.

9. If your child insists upon keeping company or finally marrying someone of whom you disapprove, you must ask for spiritual self-control by which you can make adjustments to the inevitable. Then give every support to your child's choice and believe that, all working together, good can come out of what may now seem to be a tragic circumstance.

10. I again urge you, in any situation affecting your children, to be as imperturbable as possible. Even if you are inwardly distressed, outwardly remain unperturbed. Do not show shock, disappointment, anger or disapproval. Remember that your young person is passing through a critical emotional experience and does not possess the maturity of years to give him balance. But since you do possess this asset, you are able to maintain philosophical poise. Often the situation is saved by the ability of someone to remain in absolute emotional control of himself. Of course, this power is drawn from a deep religious faith. One mother I know suggested inviting the young man in question for a week's visit during a vacation in the country. The daughter, by the end of the week, discovered characteristics in the young man she had never dreamed were there. He seemed out of place in the family circle and she herself recognised it.

11. Finally, to pray about this matter is the best assurance that it will come to a proper conclusion. If all will not pray, get as many as possible of the involved parties to participate in the prayer circle. But in the last analysis you can pray. Do not ask God to support your opinion, or anyone's, but ask Him what is the right thing to do. You will get the right answer.

An Older Person Is Living with Us, How Can We All Be Happy?

1. IT may interest you to know that in thousands of homes an older person, mother, father or in-law, is living. One doctor told me that such is the case in almost every home where he calls.

2. If the presence of an older person becomes an annoyance to you, you might reason to yourself: "Perhaps some day I, too, will have to live with my children, and I would want them to be kind and considerate to me."

3. If you are the older person in question and you become hurt at what you think is an impatience or lack of consideration, remind yourself that no matter how beloved you are, the fact remains that the family unit most naturally and fundamentally includes only husband, wife and children. Others, however dear, cannot in the nature of things be in the inner essence of that circle. A frank facing of this fact, together with the practice of consideration by every party, will help to mitigate this fundamentally unnatural arrangement.

4. Younger people will do well to emphasise the thought

that an older person in the home can conceivably add an element of quiet helpfulness and faith and thereby contribute to a finer atmosphere that will affect all.

5. The older person in the home should be extremely careful not to intrude his or her opinion in any assertive or querulous manner, but let the mother and father regulate their own home as they see fit.

6. The older person must make a life for herself or himself. Do not depend upon your children or grandchildren to entertain you or give you attention. Get as many and as varied outside interests as you can. Make your own friends and go out with them often. Make your life so interesting, so busy and important that the others in the household will admire you and be eager to know all about it. A must for an older person is an engagement book.

7. If you are ill or infirm and cannot put the foregoing into practice, read books, write letters, work with your hands, keep your mind alert, familiarise yourself with contemporary happenings such as politics, church, art, music, fashions. In other words, be so interesting that the others will be glad to have you around, sick or well.

8. At all costs, and with God as your helper, do not complain or whine or seek attention. This is the way to sure unpopularity, no matter how dearly your loved ones love you.

9. Let the younger members of the family remember that God has permitted their elderly person to remain with them while other people have missed that blessing in life. Dwell upon the privilege of walking the pathway of life together, and count every day precious because every day is one less in which to talk and love. Remember that you have memories together and your lives are intertwined, for they come from the same roots. When this is gone it will be

like a great tree falling and leaving an empty place against the sky.

10. Any home can be a place of peace and happiness if it is a home of prayer. Always say grace at table and frequently call upon the older one to pray. The prayers of older people have a quality and depth with which younger people need to be familiar.

My Children Are Not Doing Well in School

---

1. IF your children are not doing well at school there is, in all probability, a very basic, though perhaps simple reason. We will assume that it is not lack of ability or mental capacity, but that the ability and mental capacity are not being released and utilised. Always hold before your child the idea that he has untapped resources within him, and then help him to release them.

2. It may be that your child has not been taught orderly, disciplined habits of study and work. There must be regular

times to study and the work must be attacked in an orderly, systematic manner. There ought to be no deviation from this study programme; no radio programme, television show or any "special" situations, unless of extreme importance, should break regularity of the study schedule.

3. The child should be taught the psychology of confidence. He must believe in himself, that he can do his work and do it well. One way to attain this confidence is to teach him to pray about his studies. A child who starts out in life with a feeling of partnership with God in his school work will know that he cannot fail, because he has undefeatable resources. Furthermore, this faith will keep him calm and unexcited in the presence of a test or examination.

4. Whatever you do, never tell a child that he hasn't it in him, that he isn't as bright as some other boy or an older brother or sister. Never compare him with another child, thereby giving him a feeling that if he doesn't do as well he is inferior. Simply encourage him to do his best to get his work done as completely as possible, to leave nothing undone, to catch up all ragged ends. In other words, teach him efficiency within himself. Get him to compete not with others, but with himself.

5. Try to develop an atmosphere of peace, serenity and quietness in the home. Parents do not realise the effect of argument, fighting and a disturbed atmosphere on a child. This unhappy spirit develops a profound attitude of insecurity which impedes the flow of emotional and intellectual force. Make a home in which a child can develop normally and where his natural abilities will flower out. To attain this atmosphere we strongly recommend family prayer, church-going and, more important even than that, a dedication on the part of the parents to the spirit of Christ. In this

sort of home are generated love attitudes. Many children freeze up because they develop either the conscious or unconscious reaction that they are not loved, that they are rejected. They complain that nobody pays any attention to them nor takes them anywhere. They have a feeling that they struggle alone. A child surrounded by love, faith, respect, normal attention, co-operation and prayer will be freed from psychological conflicts, thus allowing his powers to bear forcibly upon his responsibilities.

6. Every evening one of the parents or both should give as much time as possible to a discussion with the child concerning his studies. The parents must never actually do the work, but concentrate on teaching the child to think. This mere show of interest by the parent is in itself a demonstration of love and reassures the child, giving him a sense of confidence.

7. A prayer with the child every night in which the next school day is successfully affirmed will send the child to sleep with the conviction of success germinating within him. Do not send the child to school with the injunction, "You must outdistance all the others because your father or mother did." Do not try to force any child to be the top student. Simply encourage him always to do honest, conscientious and complete work. Urge him to do his job just as well as he can without any reference to how anyone else did. Never tell a child that he should be ashamed of himself or that he is bringing shame upon you because he is not doing well. This will fill him with nervous fear. Constantly suggest the creative thought that if he has faith nothing is impossible unto him.

8. Pray for the child every morning and evening in this manner: "I thank you, Lord, for this child. Help him to see God in me. Let me be a stimulus to him to be God's child

with God's powers operating in him. Let him know of my faith in him. I paint on my mind a picture of my child as realising his best self and greatest powers through God's help."

PART FOUR
Spirit Lifters

PART FOUR
Spirit Lifters

Do you ever experience a "let-down" feeling? At times does your interest in life sink to a low ebb? Do you ever feel lacking in zest and enthusiasm?

Doubtless most people must sadly answer these questions in the affirmative. The problem of keeping oneself on a high level of interest, anticipation, zest is a definite one.

A decline of interest in life is often due to a creeping dullness that spreads throughout the thoughts and attitudes. Pressure, tension, anxiety, overstress, all of these deplete energy. As energy sags, responsive interest in things, events, conditions and situations declines.

When our thoughts grow tired we develop a weariness point of view. Sometimes a person will experience a succession of cruel blows such as the loss of a loved one, disappointment in an ambition, money problems, ill treatment of one kind or another. These knock the supports from under life.

Thus we might continue to recite reasons for low spirits. But, we are interested in something of a positive nature—how to lift the spirit so that we may be effective, happy and useful.

Some years ago I discovered that an effective way to keep perpetually alert, eager and enthusiastic is something so simple that it is astonishing anyone could miss it.

I found that by simply memorising certain statements from the Bible, holding them in mind and repeating them, I could re-stimulate and refresh my mind.

The Bible makes a striking statement about the power of

the words of Jesus. "If ye abide in me, and my words abide in you, ye shall ask what ye will, and it shall be done unto you" (John 15:7). I took this literally to mean that by "dropping" dynamic and refreshing sentences from the Scriptures into a mind that was tired, weary and apathetic, it would release a force able to change the condition of that mind with powerful effect.

You have seen the part of this book entitled THOUGHT CONDITIONERS, in which are listed forty passages of Scripture that can recondition the mind. The most astonishing and amazing testimonies have come from people who have used these passages as directed. One New York business-man, for example, is never without copies of them in his pocket. He showed them to me. They are soiled and dog-eared. But he says they have so revitalised his thought-processes that they saved his business and changed his life.

In this Part, SPIRIT LIFTERS, I have listed thirty-one additional Scripture statements, one for every day of the month. These have been chosen because I, and others too, have found them particularly designed to lift one out of discouraged, jaded, depressed attitudes.

The effect of a Scripture passage, when properly used, is more powerful than any other combination of words. There is presented here a system for the definite application of these powerful texts which can, if you carefully follow the suggestions given, provide you with a never-failing SPIRIT LIFTER.

SUGGESTED METHOD FOR USING
SPIRIT LIFTERS

1. Read this part from beginning to end, without interruption if possible, so as to absorb the idea of its general purpose.

2. Then read one SPIRIT LIFTER each day, and only one, for thirty-one consecutive days. Make a sincere attempt to commit each to memory. That which is thus memorised lodges permanently in the subconscious and sends off a healing and renewing potency. An idea or thought firmly lodged in the subconscious becomes determinative, for it is from the subconscious that our lives are directed.

3. As many times as possible during the day, say the passage over to yourself, aloud if possible, savouring its meaning and feeling it drive deep within your nature.

4. Once each day look for an opportunity to repeat the passage to someone else. And, if you feel guided, try to outline its meaning to that person. This is suggested because what you give to another not only benefits him, but comes back to you with threefold power.

5. Every night as you go to sleep affirm the following: "THE SPIRIT LIFTER that I read and committed today lies deeply embedded in my mind. It is now sending off throughout my thoughts its healing, refreshing effects."

6. Constantly conceive of yourself as "saturating" your mind with these creative, dynamic, life-changing thoughts. Slowly but surely this process will make of you a new person.

REALISE the power that is within you and you will no longer be a victim of depressed spirit.

And what is this inner power? Simply the God-given ability to believe. To the extent to which you develop this faculty you will master the defeats of this life. The great issue is to learn to believe.

This is stated in one of the most important of all Scripture passages.

> **Jesus said unto him, if thou canst believe, all things are possible to him that believeth.** Mark 9:23

Learn to believe. Learn to cast out doubt.

This is done by the practice of affirmation. Affirm faith, think positively, visualise achievement. Never think doubt. Always think faith.

This text does not mean necessarily that you can have everything you want. Yet it is true that, the stronger your faith, the more nearly you can attain your heart's desire.

The text does say, however, that when you learn to believe, the area of the impossible is vastly reduced and the area of the possible greatly increased.

If you set this text firmly at the centre of your thought pattern you will never again be a victim of low spirits.

Wᴇ read in the Bible of the marvellous things Jesus did for people, and rather wistfully wish that the same experience might be ours. Through faith in Jesus Christ they were able to accomplish most astonishing achievements, or were rescued from sad plights, or gained tremendous new power over difficulties.

Rather sadly we ask, "Why cannot that happen to me?"

It can, and as proof I urge you to meditate upon this tremendous Spirit Lifter.

> **Jesus Christ, the same yesterday, and today, and for ever.**   Hebrews 13:8

The simple truth here stated is that Jesus Christ never changes. He is an invariable factor in a variable world. He alone, of all men, is not a prisoner of His date. He is just the same now as when He walked the shores of Galilee. He has the same kindness, the same power to heal and change men's lives. He is the same restorer of courage, the same transformer of men's souls.

Anything that He ever did for anybody throughout all history He can do for you. It all depends upon how completely you surrender yourself to Him, and how sincerely you believe.

A REMARKABLE SPIRIT LIFTER is a verse which suggests how to obtain the values which make one's life rich and full; such as peace, quietness, material necessities, right relationships, and other good things.

The formula is in the following text:

> **But seek ye first the Kingdom of God, and his righteousness; and all these things shall be added unto you.**
>
> Matthew 6:33

First we are told to seek the Kingdom of God, a state of existence characterised by the attributes we associate with God: strength, integrity, protection, goodness, faith, love. Seek to be that way and good things will come your way.

Also, we are told to have God's righteousness, meaning right-mindedness. Learn to think right, develop a right thought pattern. Right thinking is thinking that is governed by intelligence, is positive not negative, unselfish not self-centred, creative not destructive, kindly not hateful. It is to think God's thoughts after Him.

Employ these attitudes and all "these things"—that is everything that you need for the good life—shall be added, indeed multiplied for you.

I USED to be troubled by feelings of insecurity. Uncertainties sometimes had a rather frightening effect and there was often a hesitation about going forward, especially from the known to the unknown.

I was helped to overcome this unhappy feeling by these reassuring words:

> And, behold, I am with thee, and will keep thee in all places whither thou goest, ... I will not leave thee, until I have done that which I have spoken to thee of.
>
> Genesis 28:15

The strengthening fact here expressed is that God will be with you wherever you go or in whatever situation you find yourself. It means you are never alone. He is always with you.

Moreover, the verse gives assurance that He will guide and aid you to a successful outcome of anything He has inspired you to undertake.

So, say this text over to yourself until you *know* that He is with you and will see you through.

A PROMINENT scholar and a well-known physician, in a joint article, asked this curious question. Are you happy enough to live long? They assert that 35 to 50 per cent. of all ill are sick because they are basically unhappy.

For this condition a medicine is offered in these words:

A merry heart doeth good like a medicine.

Proverbs 17:22

Joy has great therapeutic or healing value, whereas gloom and depression dry up creative life processes. Perhaps this is why Jesus so emphatically tells us to rejoice. One should learn to live the joy way. This does not mean, of course, to take a light or flippant view of the pain and realistic difficulties of contemporary life. But it does mean, certainly, to take a hopeful and optimistic attitude.

One can think happy thoughts, say happy things, and seek in every way to put joy into people's lives. The more enthusiastically you do this, the more strength you will give to others, the better you will help to make the world, and the more surely you will keep your own spirit high.

When low of spirit repeat this verse until its vitality lifts your depression.

I HAVE seen many people experience inner cleanness and thereby become spiritually refreshed through the following verse:

Now ye are clean through the word which I have spoken unto you.   John 15:3

This SPIRIT LIFTER tells us that the words spoken by Jesus Christ have a strange and mystic power, so much so that if His words are recorded in consciousness and are held there and are underscored and emphasised, you can do any worthy thing with yourself.

As the Bible puts it, "Ye shall ask what ye will and it shall be done unto you."

How can the words of Jesus Christ cleanse an individual and bring about so great a result? The answer is by teaching him to ask and receive forgiveness from wrong thoughts and actions; by changing his thoughts from impure to wholesome thinking. By filling his mind with faith, one experiences a truly marvellous brain washing whereby he becomes "whiter than snow".

By practising the teaching of love which Jesus Christ speaks of, the ugliness of hate is washed from the mind. Through confession to God and faith in Christ all sins are forgiven. They no longer have a hold upon you. The inner cleanness thus gained is an amazing source of high spirits.

SCARCELY any joy equals the realisation that you have it in you to meet all your responsibilities. This consciousness contributes immeasurably to high spirit and happiness. It is quite difficult, on the contrary, to face each day with a sense of inability and weakness. With such an attitude, life seems too much and profound discouragement sets in.

Here is the antidote to such a dismal feeling.

> **Fear thou not; for I am with thee: be not dismayed; for I am thy God: I will strengthen thee; yea, I will help thee; yea, I will uphold thee with the right hand of my righteousness.**   Isaiah 41:10

This is a most important promise which God makes to us. No matter how awesome your problems, you need have no fear. Certainly you are not to let anything dismay you, for God says He will strengthen and help you. In fact, He promises He will hold you up and make you adequate for any situation.

Accept this great fact. Hold this verse strongly in consciousness until it sends its ruggedness throughout your entire life.

THE spirit must be revitalised even as the body. And we cannot keep our spirits high by supplying them only with inspiration of a worldly nature.

The beauty of the earth, the wonders of the sky, lovely music, inspiring art, all have a profoundly inspiring effect, but leave us still seeking that which perpetually satisfies.

To meet this need we have an amazing formula for continuous revitalisation:

> **But whosoever drinketh of the water that I shall give him shall never thirst; but the water that I shall give him shall be in him a well of water springing up into everlasting life.**   John 4:14

This passage tells us that every longing of the human spirit finds enduring satisfaction in the life-giving message of Jesus. Its effect upon the spirit is to tap deep resources in the subconscious, that deep place in our souls where God resides. Thus it becomes a perpetual well of self-renewing inspiration. In this way our spirit is endowed with a continuously automatic re-stimulation. We never thirst again.

FOR anyone who wishes to enjoy life and experience God's goodness and be happy, respected and, in short, live a full, rich life read slowly, but reflectively, and, may I add, humbly, the following verses:

> **For he that will love life, and see good days, let him refrain his tongue from evil, and his lips that they speak no guile:**
>
> **Let him eschew evil, and do good; let him seek peace, and ensue it.** I Peter 3:10, 11

In these two verses are listed just a few things that put happiness in your heart.

We are told to curb our tongues from speaking evil about anyone. Simply never say anything to hurt anyone. Moreover, we are to refrain from double talk, from shrewd and canny remarks that are designed to advance our interests at someone's disadvantage. We are to turn our back upon evil, and in every way possible, do good, help people and bring blessings into their lives. We are to seek peace on the earth and in our own hearts, and so live that peacefulness may flow from us to others. We are to become an island of peace in a world of turmoil.

Do the simple, honest Christian things and life will be good and you will love it.

THE status of our relations with other people has a marked effect on our spirits. When we are on the "outs" with people or in conflict with them and a state of estrangement exists, it greatly tends to depress us.

The cure is found in this wise advice.

Be kindly affectioned one to another with brotherly love; in honour preferring one another.   Romans 12:10

The technique herein taught is simply the practice of kindly affection. Always take a generous and forbearing attitude, assuming that basically the other individual is really a fine person and that he does not mean to be as he seems. By the practice of such considerateness you can finally lift kindliness into affection and from that to the ultimate in personal relationship where you put the other person ahead of yourself. This, of course, is that supreme quality of courtesy which has an amazing power to dissipate ill-will.

The result is to free your heart of all jealousy and ill will. The love you give will return in good measure and your spirits will be lifted to new levels of joy.

TENSION is one of the worst of all depressants of the spirit. A prolonged, high-tempo pattern of thinking and living draws off energy, leaving the spirit fagged and dull. Therefore, the mind needs to experience a depth of quietness in which tension will subside.

One of the most effective passages in producing such a state of mind is the statement which follows:

Be still, and know that I am God.   Psalm 46:10

In these words is a most effective technique of relaxation. "Be still"—that is, reduce your activity, stop your headlong rush, slow down, do not walk or talk so fast; in fact, do not walk or talk at all. Sit still, be silent, let composure creep over you. You are agitated and therefore momentarily incapable of those creative and basic thoughts which can reorganise your activity.

Having attained an attitude of stillness, the greatest of all thoughts will then come stealing into your mind. You are then ready to know that "I am God"—that is, you realise that you cannot do everything, that the world does not rest on your shoulders. The simple truth that you are to do your best and leave the rest to God comes back to your consciousness. Out of such self-treatment your spirit will be lifted.

O NE effective way to get your spirits lifted is to have
fellowship with those who have lifted minds. Continued
association with negative individuals is bound to infect you
with negativism and gloom. Pessimistic conversation which
reeks with doubt and despair is bound to seep into your
consciousness and darkly colour it.

Here then is the remedy:

> **For where two or three are gathered together in my name,**
> **there am I in the midst of them.** Matthew 18:20

Arrange for periodic times of spiritual fellowship whereby
you may think and talk and pray with a few people who,
like yourself, are seeking a deeper relationship with Jesus
Christ. This practice will bring you one of the most glorious
experiences in life. You will be aware that Jesus Christ is
in the midst of such a group, and the warmth and uplift-
ment this knowledge will bring to your heart is impossible to
describe.

Try putting spiritual fellowship into your next dinner-
party, or when in conversation with cherished friends. If
you do not know such people, look for them in church.
You will find them there.

WHEN you attain a sense of undefeatability you will always be high spirited. Spirit is taken out of you when you allow yourself to be overwhelmed, nonplussed and defeated by the circumstances and conditions of daily living. The secret is to get yourself firmly based on spiritual understanding, on faith and goodness. Then nothing can defeat you.

This is described in one of the most picturesque and powerful passages in the Bible.

> **Therefore whosoever heareth these sayings of mine, and doeth them, I will liken him unto a wise man, which built his house upon a rock.**   Matthew 7:24

This passage tells us that if we accept and live by the sayings of Jesus Christ we will become like that wise man who built his house upon a rock against which the storms beat in vain. Haven't you known unshakable people like that? They have an inner serenity, strength, courage and wisdom that defy all the storms of life. Probably, like yourself, such people were once weak and beaten by life's difficulties. But they listened to Christ and were made strong.

You can be that way, too. You can be just as undefeatable. Simply "hear" and "do" as Christ says. How your spirit will rise!

OUR spirits rise when we learn *how* to receive the abundance of good things God wants to give us. The secret is in two verses:

> And I say unto you, Ask, and it shall be given you; seek, and ye shall find; knock, and it shall be opened unto you.
>
> For every one that asketh receiveth; and he that seeketh findeth; and to him that knocketh it shall be opened.
>
> Luke 11:9, 10

Note that the word *ask* is immediately followed by the words "shall be given"; that directly after the word *seek* are the words "ye shall find"; and that quickly after the word *knock* is assurance that "it shall be opened unto you". It is to emphasise that *everyone* that asketh receiveth, and *everyone* that seeketh findeth, and to *all* who knock the storehouse is opened.

Therefore confidently ask, then visualise yourself as now receiving; seek, then affirm that you *have* found; knock, then believe that God's storehouse *is* opened.

Practise receiving. Believe that you *have* been given. Then feel your spirits lift as you realise that God's blessings are actually showered upon you.

Not a little low-spirit trouble is traceable to a lack of rest. To keep the spirits high one must find renewal and refreshment of body, mind and soul. Weariness is a condition in which fatigue germs generate. And fatigue siphons off exuberance.

Therefore, it is imperative to know how to sleep, for sleep is the great restorer.

Here is a little gem from the Psalms which is a workable formula.

> **I laid me down and slept; I awaked; for the Lord sustained me.**
> Psalm 3:5

In these few simple words is a marvellous picture. It is of a man who, at the end of day, simply lay down and went to sleep. Like a child in its naturalness, his finely attuned emotional system went instantly into repose.

Then the writer of the Psalms says "I awaked." You have the picture of a man wide awake, eager and ready to meet the day. He is full of high spirits. And this is because he had a feeling that the Lord was watching over him, sustaining and protecting him.

Tonight when you go to bed practise this passage. You, too, will find restful sleep and awaken with your spirit lifted.

ONE of the most rewarding techniques is how to control anger. Admittedly, getting mad is something in which no wise person indulges because of its bad effect upon him and its harmful results in personal relations.

But beyond this, anger is a depressant of the spirit. So much energy is expended in violent anger that one is quite spent when the storm passes. The after effect is usually one of despondency and lifelessness.

Anger that is less violent but which simmers and seethes is even more depressing because it permits a constant leakage of energy.

Fortunately there is a very effective method for correcting this condition. It requires practice, but once you acquire this skill you will be amazed at the self-control it gives.

A soft answer turneth away wrath: but grievous words stir up anger.   Proverbs 15:1

The next time you feel anger rising repeat this verse several times and note the effect. It is a golden key to successful human relations and one of the best SPIRIT LIFTERS.

THE human spirit, like the good earth, must experience times of refreshment else life becomes barren, unfruitful, even bleak.

To guard against or correct such a condition meditate upon a great verse:

> Repent ye therefore, and be converted, that your sins may be blotted out, when the times of refreshing shall come from the presence of the Lord.   Acts 3:19

The earth suffers periods of diminished rainfall, sometimes for months or even years in extremely arid regions. Thus we have our dust-bowls and desert areas. Then come the cool fresh rains and the miracle of earth's renewal. It is, indeed, in the picturesque phrase of the text, a "time of refreshing".

A similar process occurs in human life. By our wrong thinking and misdeeds, the delightful freshness of mind and soul fades. Our souls are all but suffocated by dust, barrenness and deadness.

If we put ourselves in God's hands and are spiritually changed, "times of refreshing shall come from the presence of the Lord". How clean, fresh and delightful life then becomes! It is as if we had never really lived before.

HAVE you a strength renewer when you feel down and spent? Life sometimes seems almost too much for us. Here is a marvellous renewing agent, a true SPIRIT LIFTER.

He giveth power to the faint; and to them that have no might he increaseth strength. Isaiah 40:29

People, completely lacking in vitality, have passed those words through their minds and gained an amazing revitalisation. God is the source of all energy: in the sun, in plants and in people.

Truly turn your mind to Him and, through the channel of spiritual thought, He will pour new energy and strength into you. You will feel it physically, emotionally and mentally.

Once every day, perhaps twice, or even more often, practise the following renewal technique:

Lie down and completely relax. Then conceive of our Lord as touching you. Affirm that He is sending into your being His illimitable strength. With faith repeat today's SPIRIT LIFTER. You will soon feel new strength.

IN maintaining high spirits it is important to cultivate the attitude of spiritual surrender—that is, mentally to place yourself, all your interests, hopes and purposes, completely in the hands of God.

One should, of course, utilise all his powers and energy in his daily life and strive diligently to attain his objectives. But one should add to this a humble dependence on God's guidance and ever keep in harmony with His will.

This important method of living is outlined in the following passage:

> Humble yourselves therefore under the mighty hand of God, that he may exalt you in due time:
>
> Casting all your care upon him; for he careth for you.
>
> I Peter 5:6, 7

The verses tell us that if we surrender ourselves to the direction of God, being guided by His mighty hand, He will exalt us—that is, help us to attain our purposes and rise above all our defeats.

We must learn to cast all of our care upon God, and be happy in the satisfying knowledge that He cares for us. This is a supreme SPIRIT LIFTER.

I<small>N</small> counselling with people who seek help in meeting life more effectively, it is strikingly evident that their basic need is simply to find God.

A physician once told me that a large percentage of his patients did not need medicine so much as they needed God.

Tolstoy said, "To know God is to live."

How does one find God? The answer is a simple one.

> **And ye shall seek me, and find me, when ye search for me with all your heart.** Jeremiah 29:13

Say those words over and over until your mind deeply accepts the fact that God will come into your life when you want Him with all your heart.

The moment you are willing to give your whole self and surrender your life, your loved ones, your business, your problems, your health into His hands, He will come to you and help you as you have never dreamed it possible. God gives Himself to the profoundly sincere and to the deeply desiring.

Show me a man who really knows God and I will show you a happy, enthusiastic and vital man.

FEAR haunts the minds of so many people. It is a grievous malady. The Bible contains many verses that are antidotes to fear. One that has greatly helped me is the following:

> The Lord is my light and my salvation; whom shall I fear? The Lord is the strength of my life; of whom shall I be afraid?
>
> Psalm 27:1

The significant fact about this verse is that fear always lurks among shadows. It thrives in darkness. A spiritually darkened mind is a breeding ground for terrifying fears. But when you flood the darkness with light, fears scurry away. When the mind is filled with the presence of the Lord, the mind is automatically filled with light and therefore fears are driven off.

Fears also develop when one feels weak. Weakness inevitably makes one afraid. But when you fill your mind with the presence of the Lord, He transmits to you a feeling of confidence and strength. Result? You now feel quietly adequate, you are afraid of nothing.

TROUBLED feelings and the sense of depression are sometimes due to the presence of evil in the thoughts and
actions. It is a strange, sad fact that wrong thinking and
doing so agitate the spirit that restlessness and weariness
result, and accordingly one's spirit sags.

In such cases I have frequently asked the troubled and
unhappy individual to meditate on the following:

> The wicked are like the troubled sea, when it cannot rest,
> whose waters cast up mire and dirt.
>
> There is no peace, saith my God, to the wicked.
>
> Isaiah, 57:20, 21

This self-caused inner tumult keeps every dirty thing in
the human mind in a state of suspension. Thus the waters
of the soul are discoloured. No one can ever experience
inner peace until he also experiences inner cleansing.

But this condition can be corrected. The soul can be
purified by purifying the thoughts, by forgiveness, and by
the healing touch of the Great Physician.

Our souls are restless until they find peace in God.

W̲E̲ become low-spirited when we weakly give in to various temptations. It is impossible to yield to a temptation and not suffer to some degree a loss of self-respect.

Such defeat always tends to dull the spirit. It subtracts that keen sense of happiness one enjoys when in full control of self. The repetition of such defeat is perhaps the most certain means of taking the joy out of life.

One verse outlines the technique for meeting and overcoming temptation.

> **There hath no temptation taken you but such as is common to man: but God is faithful, who will not suffer you to be tempted above that ye are able; but will with the temptation also make a way to escape, that ye may be able to bear it.** I Corinthians 10:13

You need never be morally defeated. If you are tempted there is always provided a means for overcoming the temptation.

Sincerely want God's help. Then simply, earnestly ask for it, believe you have it, act as you know God wants you to do.

Victory over temptation will make you very happy and high spirited.

WHEN you keep your mind filled with thoughts of God, and actively follow the teachings of Christ, practising consistently the mental attitude of trust, a strange and wonderful experience is yours. The unmistakable feeling develops that you are watched over, protected and guided. There will be so many evidences of this fact, that no doubt can exist that the everlasting goodness hovers over you.

Let the following words sink deeply into your consciousness and this experience of God's protection will be yours.

> **For he shall give his angels charge over thee, to keep thee in all thy ways.** Psalm 91:11

How your spirit will rise, the more emphatically the sublime truth grips you that nothing in this world can hurt you. No pain, nor hardship, nor opposition, nor death itself can really harm you for God is watching over you to keep you in *all* your ways. He omits no circumstance; nor does He qualify the assurance that His amazing kindness surrounds you always.

So you can go through this world with high-hearted spirit. Believe it, for it is a great fact, God watches over you.

DEPRESSION of spirit is often caused by a haunting sense of incompleteness and by unresolved conflicts. Nature is constantly making a strong effort to attain wholeness or completeness within us and to heal abrasions in the soul. Not a little physical and emotional difficulty arises from these unhappy divisions within the self.

Jesus Christ is the skilful Physician who is able to heal the personality and bring to it unification and completeness.

This is described in a wonderful passage.

> And whithersoever he entered, into villages, or cities, or country, they laid the sick in the streets, and besought him that they might touch if it were but the border of his garment: and as many as touched him were made whole.
>
> Mark 6:56

To experience His healing power simply, with all your heart, want Him to touch you. Then yield yourself to Him willingly. We make the first move, however timidly it may be, and He responds with the miraculous touch that makes us whole in body, mind and spirit.

Experiment and discover for yourself how your spirits rise when you gain a deep inner sense of wholeness.

How to wage the battle of life successfully is an art that we must learn. Several verses in the sixth chapter of Ephesians give the answer.

> Above all, taking the shield of faith, wherewith ye shall be able to quench all the fiery darts of the wicked.
>
> And take the helmet of salvation, and the sword of the Spirit, which is the word of God.   Ephesians 6:16, 17

In olden days when men wore armour the shield was used to protect the heart. As the symbol and centre of life the heart must be guarded from attack. You must keep your heart sturdy with faith.

We should also wear the helmet of salvation. The knight always tried to protect his head, and so must we protect our minds against attitudes that would destroy effectiveness —namely negativism, pessimism, evil thoughts, hate. The mind must be kept clean and ever filled with positive concepts.

Third, take the sword of God's word, by which we can put to flight the enemies of the good life, wrong thinking and wrongdoing.

Thus armed we can win in the battle of life. The realisation of our strength raises and sustains our spirit.

STALENESS and barrenness result from a depletion of spiritual inspiration. Out of this uninspired condition develops tension, stress, dissatisfaction, frustration.

But there is a cure. It is outlined in one of the most famous of all passages.

> **He maketh me to lie down in green pastures: he leadeth me beside the still waters.** Psalm 23:2

Anyone who has ever travelled through a desert area is impressed when he comes finally to the green grass country. Rich lush pastures take the place of dry and barren soil. What makes the difference? Life-giving water.

In similar manner the arid condition of human personality becomes as green pastures when the water of life flows through mind and heart.

In this experience of the still waters one sees a reflection of life at its best. The peace that passeth understanding develops in the mind.

Thus the soul is restored. It becomes peaceful, and so develops new life and vitality. Meditation upon this passage will endow you with deep serenity, and lift the spirit to new heights.

PEOPLE who complain of being dispirited are frequently those who are swamped by so many things. Lacking a strong grip on God they exercise a very weak control over themselves. They give in to irritation, resentment, anxiety and to sinful practices.

People do not want to be this way. They become disgusted with themselves because they are so. But they just haven't the inner force to exercise discipline and self-control either over their problems or themselves. So, life falls away from them and they are frustrated.

To counteract this unhappy condition we have a SPIRIT LIFTER as follows:

> **He that overcometh shall inherit all things; and I will be his God, and he shall be my son.**   Revelation 21:7

The secret here contained is simply to practise the idea that you are a child of God. As such, God will be your guide and He will lend you His strength to augment your own weak force. With God's power you can then overcome instead of being overcome.

Then instead of things flowing away from you, they will flow toward you and you shall indeed "inherit all things". In a most remarkable manner life will come your way.

As a result you will get a great lift of spirit.

Low spirits often arise out of a disturbing sense of apprehension of the future. Anxiety about future well-being, about material provision for the years that lie ahead, create insecurity feelings which, when habitually entertained, tend to result in low-spiritedness.

But how the spirit rises when one develops a feeling of confidence that he will be cared for, that all will be well, that the future is bright with promise.

A verse which we would do well to embed deeply in our consciousness is the following:

> **But my God shall supply all your need according to his riches in glory by Christ Jesus.** Philippians 4:19

This gives us the conviction that if we do our part, and live right, and have faith, God will see that all of our real needs are supplied. This includes material needs, needs of the mind, of the soul, and of the spirit. God has infinite riches, enough for all of us. We can receive these through God's law of boundless supply. If we truly have faith in Him and live according to His principles we need never look in vain for the satisfaction of any necessity.

Believe this and your spirit will be lifted out of apprehension into confidence.

Sorrow over the death of a loved one is a heavy weight upon the spirit. It often causes the one who mourns to feel that life will never again be filled with high and buoyant attitudes.

But life goes on and one must live. In a sense one is not fully loyal, perhaps, to the departed loved one unless he meets life manfully, courageously, spiritually.

The passage which follows has probably brought more healing to the human soul, and given more lift to the spirit in sorrow than any other passage in all the literature of the world.

> **I am the resurrection, and the life: he that believeth in me, though he were dead, yet shall he live.**
>
> John 11:25

What a glorious message—Jesus Christ is alive and those who believe in Him live, also. So our loved one, whom we thought dead, isn't dead at all, but lives and shall forever touch our lives, watching over us with the same love and tenderness.

This gives such a lift to the spirit that one wants to shout from the house-tops the glorious fact that through faith in Jesus Christ, we live. So when sorrow comes, repeat over and over this wonderful passage. And presently the shadows will flee away and the light of a new day will dawn for you.

THE top three-point formula for worthwhile living is contained in this immortal statement.

And now abideth faith, hope, love (charity), these three; but the greatest of these is love (charity).

I Corinthians 13:13

Here you have three powerful SPIRIT LIFTERS. First is faith—faith in God, and in Christ; in yourself, in your fellowmen and in life itself. Faith is the greatest power in this world and it can be yours.

Next is hope—the attitude of expectancy, believing that the best is yet to be, that always ahead lies opportunity. Believe this and it will be so.

Finally is love—your heart filled with goodwill, not hate or resentment or ill-will, but love. And truly this is one of the greatest qualities of all, a heart filled with compassion and understanding and a desire to help people. Christian love will give you a deep joy.

Let these three attitudes shine like stars in your life and your spirit will be uplifted always.

PART FIVE
You Can Relax

I RECEIVE hundreds of letters every week as a result of my writing, radio and television work, and am appalled by the number of people who tell of tension, unrest and nervousness in their lives. I wonder if this generation has forgotten how to rest, how to take it easy.

Our Lord Jesus Christ came to teach people about the abundant life. To possess this quality of life one must have peace of mind, and something that is even deeper than that —peace of soul. Inner serenity, mind and soul quietness can counteract the ill effects of this troubled world.

As long as an inner quiet centre is maintained, one will be able to draw upon resources to keep him steady and effective, however many storms he may encounter.

We do not teach relaxation in order that one may enter into a selfish quietude and retreat from life, shutting himself up in some isolated ivory tower. We teach relaxation of body, mind and soul so that one may enter vigorously into life's responsibilities and opportunities—but without breaking himself. Only the relaxed person can meet life efficiently.

Now how to use this technique:

1. Read Part Five through from beginning to end, without stopping if possible. This will give you a complete picture of its plan and scope.

2. Then select the one lesson that made the greatest appeal to you. Re-read and study that lesson and follow the

instructions given. Please remember, this is not a "reading" book but a book of practice. Sincerely follow the suggestions given and you will get results.

3. Next, take the chapters day by day in order. In the two weeks' time for which this series is designed, you should have some new insights as to how you can improve yourself emotionally.

4. For the person who does not admit to feeling tense, who seems perfectly calm and peaceful, these principles may still be of value. Use the book as a bedside devotional guide, or as a morning spiritual exercise. Its use may serve as a tension preventative.

5. I should like to point out that here, as in all of my writings, I endeavour to use simple, everyday language and avoid traditional religious phraseology. This must not be taken to mean that we do not lay supreme stress on the efficacy of the teachings of Jesus Christ. We merely want to make these precepts understandable to the greatest number of people, many of whom are unfamiliar with so-called religious language.

6. To the extent to which you believe and practise and surrender yourself to the control of Christ over your personality, will you find inner quietness, rest and relaxation. Jesus stated an absolute truth when He said, "Come unto me . . . , and *I* will give you rest."

Drain Your Mind

THE average man, before retiring, usually empties his pockets on to his dresser or desk. Personally, I rather enjoy standing over a waste-paper basket during this process to see how many things I can throw away: notes, memos, scraps of paper, completed self-directions, even knick-knacks which I have picked up. With relief I deposit all items possible in the waste-paper basket.

It occurred to me one night that I ought to empty my mind as I empty my pockets. During the day we pick up many mental odds and ends: a little worry, a little resentment, a few annoyances, some irritations perhaps even some guilt reactions. Every night these should be drained off, for unless eliminated they accumulate.

And how do you drain the thoughts? I suggest that you think of your mind as a wash-basin with a stopper in the bottom. Mentally remove the stopper and imaginatively "see" the mass of soiled material disappear down the drain. Then mentally replace the stopper and fill the mind with clean, wholesome, spiritual thoughts.

You must be careful in performing this process not to take a thought back. When you have drained it out, conceive of it as gone. If your mind attempts to reach out for the old thought, stop it by saying, "That is gone forever, removed by God's Grace, and I will not take it back."

One night I came home to find my wife, ever the perfect housekeeper, experimenting with some new appliances for her vacuum cleaner. She showed me a long arm attachment with which dust could be sucked out of hidden corners.

While admiring this mechanical gadget it occurred to me that a similar spiritual mechanism could be employed to draw "dust" out of our thoughts.

So I developed for myself a vacuum-cleaner prayer: "Dear Lord, by the power of Thy spirit draw now from the unseen crannies and crevices of my soul the dust of the world which has settled there."

Try this. The resulting sense of cleanness will add to your inner peace.

Another method is to figuratively and imaginatively reach into your mind, as though you could put your fingers into your brain and lift out unhappy thoughts one by one. As you imagine yourself doing this, affirm: "I am now taking out and throwing away that fear, that prejudice, that resentment, that impure recollection." Then when the mind is thus emptied affirm: "I am now putting into my mind the pure thoughts of Christ. I am asserting the love of God, the goodness of our Lord."

Before you have even completed this process the kindly heavenly Father, who is pleased when His children thus deal with themselves, will have enfolded you in His kindly peace.

Relax Muscle Tensions

To rest efficiently it is necessary to know how to relax muscle tensions.

One effective method is to practise thinking generously. If someone has not treated you "right" just think some generous thoughts about him and see how quiet it makes you feel. Resentful, ill-will thoughts tighten you up. Generous thoughts loosen your entire nervous mechanism.

In addition, I suggest a relaxation technique developed by the famous psychiatrist, Dr. Smiley Blanton. (This is more fully outlined in *The Art of Real Happiness* by Peale and Blanton.*)

1. As you lie on your bed spend a moment or two clenching your hands and opening them. Double your fists and make a circular motion with them. To relax a physical member it is first necessary to exercise it. The hands and the forearms are centres of tension.

*Published by The World's Work.

2. Raise to your shoulders your clenched fists, extend your arms and make circular motions with the shoulders.

3. Raise your arms and allow them to fall limply to your sides as though you had no muscular control over them. The more limp you can make them, the more truly relaxed they are becoming.

4. Without moving your legs stretch your toes in the direction of your head as far as you can do so, then extend them as far as possible away from you. This exercises the muscles of the lower legs.

5. Bring up one knee as closely as possible to your chest and then extend it fully, doing the same with the other knee. Repeat several times. Exercise the abdominal muscles by sitting up and lying back several times. Use your hands as little as possible in raising yourself.

6. Still reclining, raise your head from the pillow as far as possibly and allow it to fall back limply. Do this several times. Allow one leg to swing freely over the side of the bed, thinking of it as hinged. Repeat the movement with the other leg.

7. Again reclining, breathe deeply in and out several times. A deep breath tends to contract the diaphragm, and when quickly expelled assists in relieving tension.

8. Upon completing these exercises lie quietly, allowing your mind to touch upon every member of your body, at the same time thinking of each part as becoming more and more relaxed. This will induce deeper levels of relaxation.

9. Finally, think of some very restful scene: hills shrouded in a misty haze of blue; a wood-thrush singing; the far-off distant whistle of a train among the hills; soft moonlight over a white-faced meadow; the loving and eternal face of God.

These relaxation suggestions may be practised at intervals

during the day or before retiring at night. Hundreds of people have found them effective in producing a state of quietness and rest.

❖❖❖❖❖❖❖❖❖❖❖❖❖❖❖❖❖❖❖❖❖❖❖❖❖❖❖❖❖❖❖❖❖❖

Don't Take Tomorrow to Bed with You

❖❖❖❖❖❖❖❖❖❖❖❖❖❖❖❖❖❖❖❖❖❖❖❖❖❖❖❖❖❖❖❖❖❖

I KNEW a man who complained of being a poor sleeper. We analysed his daily and nightly habits and discovered that after he got to bed he took a pad and pencil and made a series of notes about what he was going to do the next day. He planned out tomorrow, making an outline of each problem or responsibility that was to be handled.

He prided himself on this "efficiency" method which he had developed, and considered it a unique procedure.

He placed the pad and pencil on his night table and would often reach for them in the darkness, adding additional memos that his restless mind supplied. He told with pride how well he had mastered the skill of writing legibly in the darkness.

Why couldn't he sleep? Simply because he was taking tomorrow to bed with him.

We, too, believe in efficiency. In fact one of our mottoes is, "plan your work and work your plan". But there is a time and place for all things, and in bed, ready to go to sleep, is certainly not the time to plan the next day. In fact, it is not efficient to do any tomorrow planning later than 9 P.M. if you are going to bed at 11 P.M.; not later than 8 P.M. if you are going to bed at 10 P.M. This interval of two hours will give the plans time to pass from the surface of the mind, where they agitate, into the deeper levels, where they become creative.

If, in sleeplessness, apprehensions of the morrow disturb you, simply remind yourself that God had helped you through every day you have lived heretofore, and that tomorrow will be no exception. Slowly repeat aloud the following line from an old hymn: "So long Thy power has blest me, sure it still will lead me on." This will convince you of God's continuing care, and thus a comforted, relaxed feeling will come.

Also repeat this passage: "Sufficient unto the day is the evil thereof." (Matthew 6:34.)

That is to say, do not concern yourself about any presumed evil thing that may happen, for if that feared day comes, it will either care for itself, or you will know how to deal with it, or God will handle it. Certainly do not take it to bed with you and let it disturb your night's sleep, for nothing can be done about it tonight.

The happy fact is that what seems to you to presage evil may very well turn out to be good. At any rate, go to sleep in the conscious thought and affirmation that whatever you may be called upon to handle the next day, God and you can and will do together. Anyway, a good night's sleep will serve to muster needed powers to meet tomorrow's responsibilities. Relax in God's protecting care. In faith and trust let God give you rest. Remember that all things work together for good to those who love and trust God.

Don't take tomorrow to bed with you.

Practise the Presence

AFTER the study and practice of spiritual techniques over many years, I feel that no one has ever improved upon the method of Brother Lawrence, saintly character of the Middle Ages. He was a humble man, a cook, but a great saint, and he found peace even in what may seem a menial and monotonous activity. His secret was the practice of the presence of God.

The method which he taught is simply to believe that always, at any hour of the day or night, in whatever circumstance or condition, Jesus Christ is actually present. At first this may seem but a beautiful fantasy, but as the idea is definitely practised it becomes an amazing and glorious reality. Not only great saints like Brother Lawrence, but everyday people have found it to be actually true. The Presence *is* with them.

When you retire, pull up a chair alongside your bed and imaginatively believe that Jesus Christ sits there beside you. This is not far-fetched for He said, "I am with you alway." (Matthew 28:20.) Talk with Him just as you would if some loved one were sitting in that chair. Ask Him all your questions, tell Him what is on your heart, then imagine what His answer would be if He spoke with the tongue of flesh. Soon you will have no doubt that He does speak with you, and you will sense and feel His presence with certainty.

The poet, Wordsworth, had the habit of imagining how it would be to talk to Jesus. What would be the look on His face, the tone of His voice? So real did Jesus become to him as a result of this practice that he actually felt the Master was his close companion and friend. So at intervals during the day, and especially at night, practise His presence and it will become real to you also.

When you especially feel the need of the presence of Christ, read His words from your Bible. It might be well to use a New Testament in which His actual words are underscored. This will enable you to read quickly His words in sequence. I have often done this, and it gives an amazing feeling that He is with one—actually talking to you. The feeling of comfort will be so profound, the actuality of His presence so tangible that you will feel deeply relaxed and at peace.

Should you be awakened in the night, I suggest that you practise the method of a friend of mine. He explains that, when awakened, he assumes the Lord wants to say something to him, knowing that he is more receptive when relaxed. "So," he said, "I simply lie quietly, letting Him speak

to me. And when He has given me His message I return
to sleep."

He reports that some of his "best ideas" have come during
such interludes of spiritualised wakefulness. That is not surprising, for ideas get through most effectively when a mind
is rested. The practice of the Presence produces creative
quietness in addition to profound inner restfulness.

Tranquillise Your Thoughts

THE process of tranquillising the mind is important in
assuring a condition of body, mind and soul that will
induce perfect rest.

John Masefield, one of the world's most famous poets,
developed in his early life a most beneficial practice of relaxation. At the close of the day's work he "practised the
getting of tranquillity". This served not only to reduce the
tension which the day had stimulated, but it also prepared
him for a satisfactory night's rest.

The emphasis upon practice is of no slight importance, for the ability to put the mind into a tranquil condition is attained only by persistent effort. Old habits of inner disturbance may be overcome by practice. Happily the mind will respond to systematic training.

The first step is deliberately to conceive of the mind as entirely quiet. Think of it as the surface of a pond on which there is not the faintest suggestion of a ripple. Picture the mind as motionless and filled with deep quietness.

Think silence until an atmosphere of silence seems to surround you. Suggest tranquil ideas to the mind, remembering that your thoughts respond to suggestion. Slowly, deliberately repeat the following words: tranquillity, serenity, peacefulness. Picture silent places: the deep woods, a lonely sea beach, a remote country road, a mountain lake at twilight. Sing or hum a hymn, the melody and words of which are of a tranquil character such as: "Drop Thy still dews of quietness, till all our strivings cease."

Practise actually "receiving" the gift of Christ's peace. Do that by repeating His words, personalised. "Peace I leave with .... (insert your first name), my peace I give unto .... (insert your first name): not as the world giveth, give I unto .... (insert your first name). Let not .... (insert your first name) heart be troubled, neither let it be afraid." (John 14:27.)

The next step in tranquillising the mind, which many people find particularly effective, is to make a mental list of the numerous times God has been good to you. It might be well to make this list on paper in order to see, as well as think, the list of God's good deeds.

As an example of His many acts of goodness, you might list recovery from an illness, the guidance that helped you take the right course when you were baffled, the time your loved one was divinely protected, the occasion when in deepest discouragement you found a way out of difficulty.

Then affirm, "Since God has helped me so many times, I will continue to count upon His amazing kindness."

Repeat this practice daily and you will be amazed by the new tranquillity of your mind.

❖❖

How to Spend the Hour Before Bedtime

❖❖

As one approaches the hours of rest certain preparations will prove beneficial.

During the last hour before retiring, deliberately prevent the mind from being agitated by problems. The cares, responsibilities and decisions of life should be put aside for the night so that mind, soul and body may be refreshed and renewed by sound, healthful sleep.

Let the mind, as far as possible, go into neutral. Affirm, "I now cease mental consideration of any problem."

Visualise all matters as being put aside. Think of any problem as being dropped deeply into the subconscious to quietly simmer until morning. When you take it up again it may be solved.

Spend the last hour preliminary to sleep in light and pleasant conversation with your loved ones.

If you live alone, select an entertaining radio or television programme, or read a carefree story.

Then spend fifteen minutes with the greatest of all books— the Bible. Some find it helpful to read a Psalm every night. Others, a chapter from the New Testament. Still others open the Bible at random, believing that by "guidance" they will find the passage best suited to their need.

After reading the Bible spend at least five minutes in relaxed meditation. Conceive of the words you have read as seeping into your mind, and picture them spreading a spiritual balm throughout your entire being—mental, emotional, physical.

In this quiescent state allow your body to adjust itself further in muscular relaxation. Continue to sit quietly, holding the thought that God is touching you with His peace.

As you undress your body to prepare for bed, also undress your mind. You would not think of climbing into bed fully dressed. But often we get into bed with our mind encumbered by all manner of unhappy thoughts. Drop off one by one these weights and impediments which the mind has carried through the day, so that it will be free of pressure and as comfortable as your body.

Before getting into bed, stand at the window and reflect on the beauty of the night. Behold the moon sailing high in the heavens, lighting up the clouds in silvery radiance. Contemplate the stars, the forget-me-nots of the angels. Or perhaps watch the snow slanting toward the earth or drifting high against the fence. Or listen to the heavy padded quietness of the fog. Or put your head out the window and let the rain fall against your face for a moment. Let the beauty and mystery of God's world make themselves felt in your thoughts. It will absorb in consciousness.

Then say your prayers and enter confidently into complete rest.

Relax by Positive Thinking

I BELIEVE that many people are poor sleepers largely because they *think* they are not going to sleep well. They go to bed not expecting to sleep. And so, having created an ineffective sleep pattern in their thoughts, it is actualised in real experience.

Thoughts are dynamic, and so great is their power that they tend actually to create the conditions pictured in thinking. This is especially true of thoughts that are habitually held. Negative thought patterns produce an atmosphere conducive to negative results. On the contrary, a positive thought pattern attracts, as by magnetic influence, every positive factor in the world about us. Positive thought actualises in positive results, even as negative thinking actualises in negative results.

Essentially, a negative thought is a picture of some unhappy outcome the mind expects to happen. Positive thought is a picture of something good that the mind fully expects will come to pass.

So powerful is the creative force of positive or negative thinking that it can induce sleep or drive it from us, it can keep us relaxed and rested or tense and tired.

So our suggestion is that on your way home from work you use the following affirmation: "I am going to have a nice dinner and a pleasant evening, and will top it off with a wonderful night's sleep."

Picture yourself as sleeping soundly all night long. As you retire affirm, "I am going to enjoy a sound and restful night, and will awaken with renewed energy and eager zest for tomorrow's activities." When you awaken in the morning, again affirm, saying, "What a satisfying sleep I had—with God's help I had a wonderful night and am completely relaxed. I feel refreshed and ready for a great day."

Apply the dynamic power of faith to your rest and relaxation problem and remember, in so doing it is very important to think positively that you are being relaxed. Recall the New Testament promise: "If ye have faith as a grain of mustard seed . . .; nothing shall be impossible unto you." (Matthew 17:20.) That means rest, as well as every other factor in your life.

In conversation never state that you are a poor sleeper, that you cannot rest or relax. It is always dangerous to affirm a negative. Not only does it adversely affect people to whom you say it, but your own subconscious accepts it.

The repeated affirmation of a negative or a positive tends to make it a fact.

Therefore, assert, "With God's help I have learned to rest. I sleep well at night, and complete refreshment is mine. I relax as I work. Rest and renewal are automatically mine, since I am always attached to God's boundless supply of energy."

Such practice will develop your relaxation capacity and help you become more expert in the restorative process which adds power to your life.

❖❖

Don't Wear Yourself Out with Yourself

❖❖

MUCH tiredness is the result of extreme self-preoccupation. Introspection, concern about comfort, prerogatives and position can consume a large share of one's energy.

I have observed that people who have the time and strength to do things in a big way give the least attention to themselves. Their wants are reduced to a minimum. They give themselves just enough time to care for physical requirements and to dress neatly. The main bulk of their

time and energy is thus available to do the important jobs in
life.

So, make a list of all the little things you do about your
own person every day, and see how much of this minutiae
you can lop off.

Become systematic. An example is the man who lays out
his underwear, socks, shirt, tie, and decides on his suit for
morning before going to bed. "Like a fireman, I get into my
regalia in half the time it formerly required," declared a man
who practises this system.

Obsessions probably cause the greatest drain on energy
of any personal disability. It is quite impossible to become
practised in relaxed living and enjoy restful rest until one
overcomes those compulsive neuroses of an obsessional
nature which drive and harass the victim.

For example, I recall a man who felt that he had to perform a complicated ritual every day. He always went back
to the wash-basin three times to be sure the water was
turned off. He tried the door three times to be sure it was
locked. He constantly worried that unless he did this or
that or some other thing a terrible thing would happen.

This poor fellow used up so much energy on these obsessions that he was a tired, worn-out man, even before he tried
to do his work.

The cure? He confessed, emptied out and received forgiveness for sinful acts. These sins, festering in the subconscious, had created a guilty feeling and stimulated the unconscious but persistent conviction that he should be
punished. So he was actually unconsciously punishing himself. The Scripture phrase describes him well. "The wicked
flee when no man pursueth." (Proverbs 28:1.) He was
actually pursuing himself to inflict punishment upon himself. A deep spiritual experience cured him. He asked for

and received forgiveness, and then God taught him how to forgive himself by accepting God's mercy with humble gratitude.

Many people are tired because of such emotional illnesses that drive them to irrational compensation for wrongdoing. So get your guilt feeling cleared up with the help of Christ. Then you can truly relax and be rested.

❖❖❖

Memorised Peacefulness

❖❖❖

ONE time in the midst of activities, which I had foolishly allowed to become hectic, I went to Atlantic City. From my window I could look out directly upon the sea as it washed gently on soft shores of sand. It was very quieting to behold this scene.

The day was overcast with drifting fog and cloud. Imperturbably the sea rolled shoreward with its deep-throated roar and ceaseless but perfect rhythm. Clean spume blew from its wave crests.

Over the beach, and climbing high against the blue sky,

and then sliding down the wind with ineffable grace, sea-
gulls soared and dived.

Everything in this scene was graceful, beautiful and
conducive to serenity. Its benign peacefulness laid a healing,
quieting touch upon me. I closed my eyes and discovered
that I could still visualise the scene just as I had beheld it.
There it was, as clear cut as when actually viewed by the
eye. It occurred to me that the reason I could "see it" with
my eyes closed was because my memory had absorbed it and
was able to reproduce it in detail.

Why then, I reasoned, could I not live again and again
in this scene of quiet beauty even though bodily absent from
the place?

I began the practice of deliberately visualising quiet
scenes of beauty in which I had once actually lived.

Sometimes in the midst of active work I have found it
profitable to stop for a minute or two and bring up out of
memory's storehouse scenes that had impressed me by their
beauty, and experience once again their remarkable power
to quiet, to soothe and to relax.

For example, I have found that when sleep comes with
difficulty, I can actually induce slumber by visualising out
of memory scenes of quietness and peace. Lying in a relaxed
manner in my bed I practise going back as far as I can
remember and recollect one by one the truly peaceful experiences of my life, such as the time I gazed upon Mont Blanc
when the vast mountain was bathed in moonlight. Or the
radiant sun-kissed morning when our great white ship
dropped anchor in the incredibly blue waters off Waikiki
Beach in Hawaii. Or that mystic evening when I first
watched the purple shadows fill the Grand Canyon to over-
flowing with hush. Or watching the sunlight sift through
ancient maple trees on to a green lawn on a summer after-

noon at my farm home. As I traversed these marvellous scenes of beauty and peace through the power of memory to recreate them, God's quietness overcame me, and I drifted into a sound and untroubled sleep.

So, now and then, let go your cares and the problems of the day, and wander in memory among the most beautiful places and scenes in which you have ever lived. This will quiet you, and as you yield yourself to the benign power of quiet visualisation you will find rest and relaxation.

❖❖

Drop Relaxing Bible Passages into the Mind

❖❖

ONE of the most effective relaxing agents is a therapeutic Bible passage "dropped" into one's agitated and tired mind. If you have never tried this, I cannot urge you too strongly to experiment with the process at once.

Most tiredness emanates from the thoughts. We become tired in the mind before becoming tired in the muscles. For example, you sink into your chair exclaiming that you are "tired to death". Then a friend comes, or an exciting fire breaks out down the street. Your new interest makes you forget you are tired.

Cares, worries, decisions, exasperations, multiplied during the day, bring the mind to the point where it wants to escape; and so it actually tells you that you are tired.

So the mind needs to be refreshed, and this is accomplished by lifting consciousness to a higher level.

To a certain extent, beautiful music, a quick change of scenery, a joke, a diverting experience will accomplish this momentarily.

But the form of thought diversion which reaches the profounder levels of consciousness most effectively is a Bible verse. Why? Perhaps because it comes from the most trusted Book. It is basic truth. It is God's word. It contains the healing power of Christ's spirit.

Probably what happens is that a Bible verse brings so much faith into your mind that it drives off weariness, for weariness is but another form of negativism.

What are some of the most effective verses, and how may they be used? The suggested method is as follows:

Repeat the verse aloud slowly. Saying the words out loud impresses them more deeply upon your consciousness by adding hearing to sight. When said slowly the full melody of the text is brought out. Moreover, each word in a Bible passage has significance, and a slow vocalisation tends to emphasise the full meaning of each separate precious word and syllable.

It is also valuable and important to commit these passages to memory and to articulate them at intervals during the day, especially when you may tend to feel a bit down or depleted in energy.

"My presence shall go with thee, and I will give thee rest." (Exodus 33:14.)

"Take my yoke upon you, and learn of me . . . : and ye shall find rest into your souls." (Matthew 11:129.)

"Rest in the Lord, and wait patiently for him: fret not thyself." (Psalm 37:7.)

"Let the peace of God rule in your hearts." (Colossians 3:15.)

"He maketh me to lie down in green pastures: he leadeth me beside the still waters. He restoreth my soul." (Psalm 23:2, 3.)

Search the Scriptures to discover for yourself other passages that seem especially meaningful to you.

The Benediction of the Darkness

CONSIDER how kindly God is in giving us darkness once in every twenty-four hours. Darkness is intended as an asset to relaxation.

Relaxation is encouraged by shutting the eyes, for when they are closed, one is in a healing darkness. At evening time the soft mantle of night is laid over the earth by the Heavenly Father, so that under its soft folds His children may experience relief from the day.

Unfortunately, many in early life become afraid of the dark.

When I was a boy, my brothers and I spent several summer seasons with my grandmother in a huge old-fashioned house. We slept in high-poster beds in a rather lonely room upstairs. As she prepared to leave us and we were a bit nervous, she would say, "Remember, boys, you are not alone. In the darkness God draws near." She then offered a prayer, one line of which I never forgot. "Oh, Lord, in the darkness watch over the pillow of these little boys this night."

Thus, we learned not to fear the dark, but actually to appreciate it. I shall never cease to be grateful for this concept of the spiritual benediction of God's kindly darkness.

Many human minds are the scene of battles which take place in the night. When one is tired, energy is of course depleted, and nerve-force spent. Accordingly, resistance is lowered. It is at this low moment that nameless fears, vague dreads and pathetic insecurities come trooping round our bed. Even as familiar objects in the room become grotesque in the darkness, so do these fears assume abnormal proportions.

It will help to think of God as a great and tender Father, softly putting His hands on your eyelids and soothing them, meanwhile saying reassuringly, "Fear not, I am with you." In the darkness affirm God's protection by using the following words, "He shall give his angels charge over thee, to keep thee in all thy ways." (Psalm 91:11.) And His angels will truly drive away your fears. These angels are especially active in the darkness, and hover protectingly all around you. Guardian angels they are called.

Also, think of the kindly figure of Christ as sitting beside you with His lamp. But the lamp is shaded, for He wants you to have the quieting benefit of His holy darkness, that you may relax and rest and sleep.

Do you remember as a child when you were ill, your mother sat in your room beside a soft shaded lamp during the long watches of the night? There was sufficient darkness to put you to sleep, but just enough light from the lamp to reflect her loving face. What a comfort it was!

Always in the darkness, watching over you, is your Heavenly Father. His angels are keeping watch, banishing all fears. Whether in darkness or light, God is always with you.

Add Up Your Blessings

TENSION and sleeplessness often come from a haunting sense of life's uncertainties.

One of the best antidotes to this unhappy condition is the practice of the therapy of thanksgiving. Begin with the immediate day just closing and work backward, listing every blessing, however small.

As they add up you will get a new understanding of the goodness of God and the extraordinary good fortune which He has given to you. You will be profoundly impressed by the certainties of your life, and as a result, your nervous un-certainties "will fold their tents like the Arabs, and as silently steal away".

What are some of the blessings which you can list as you practise this method at the close of day?

They might run somewhat as follows:

I thank God for the comfortable bed in which I shall sleep this night, that there is a good tight roof over my head. I am thankful for my loved ones and friends wherever they are. I am thankful for the good dinner I had tonight and for a good digestion. I am thankful I was able to get enough money to pay that overdue bill today. I am thankful for the good work I did in my job today.

You see, we have made only a few suggestions, and mani-festly we have not yet exhausted the simple blessings of this one day. It is very easy to enumerate the difficulties and negatives of life, and the mind has the tendency to dwell upon such. But the mind can be trained to see with equal facility the positives and all the good things with which our lives are filled.

One process creates tension, nervousness and unhappi-ness. The other induces peace, calmness and joy.

As you proceed during the day and are called upon to face certain problems, practise taking an optimistic view at all times. You will be surprised at how this attitude will help you to approach every matter in a relaxed manner. Besides, it is a fact that an optimistic approach brings to pass better results than a pessimistic view of outcomes.

This is not difficult to understand, for the optimist tends to throw his all into a proposition. The pessimist holds something of himself back and gets back less than the man who gives more of himself. This explains why relaxed people achieve more than tense persons.

The simple habit of adding up possibilities becomes important in successful living. This does not mean that one cannot be "realistic". But by and large the positive attitude is nearer the truth about life than the cautious negative approach.

So as you go through life, do not practise subtraction; but instead add up your blessings, opportunities, possibilities. In so doing you will be relaxed, outgoing and successful.

❖❖

Become an Expert Forgetter

❖❖

PRACTISING the art of forgetting has remarkable power to relax and to relieve strain. Some people complain that they have trouble memorising. Far more have trouble forgetting.

Inasmuch as many breakdowns result from overburdening the mind with unhappy memories of failure or frustration, the unburdening process of forgetting becomes of tremendous importance.

Many people lie in bed at night remembering what somebody said about them, or did to them. They are hauntingly agitated by the recollection of something left undone or done poorly. As a result of this unpleasant cogitation, their

minds, made miserably nervous, probe back into the best
forgotten past and unpleasantly dwell on old sins, old sor-
rows, old unhappiness. Thus the mind flits restlessly from
one misery centre to another, somewhat after the manner of
the bee—except that it is not taking honey from beautiful
flowers of pleasant episodes, but rather sipping dissatisfaction from the rank weeds of past experience.

A superlative aid to mental health is the Biblical statement: "Forgetting those things which are behind, and reaching forth unto those things which are before, I press toward
the mark for the prize of the high calling of God in Christ
Jesus." (Philippians 3:13, 14.)

Repeat this to yourself several times when your mind
tends to dwell on unhappy things. This will help you to
forget. And to the extent to which you master skill in forgetting, you shall enjoy untroubled sleep and energy renewing rest.

Forgetting, however, is not a negative, but a positive process. It is the effective forcing of something destructive from
the thoughts by a process of displacement. This is accomplished by the technique of substituting for unhappy
memories every pleasant incident or occurrence you can
recall. As you force your thoughts to focus on the happy
good things, the unhappy evil things will gradually fade
from consciousness, having been displaced.

I suggest that you make a sacred nightly ceremony of the
locking of your door. Stand beside your door and affirm,
"There are a lot of things that I am *now* forgetting. I ask
them to depart from my mind, for they are bad company. I
am *now* putting them outside my door and bidding them go
away. I am *now* closing the door. I *now* turn the key. The
lock clicks and they have gone."

Such continued inhospitality, persisted in nightly toward

all unhappy thoughts concerning any event of the day, will ultimately discourage such thoughts, and presently you will enjoy permanent peace. The nightly process of thought displacement will encourage the ability to select only peaceful and relaxing thoughts. In this manner, the art of forgetting develops a skill in thought control which is most important to effective living.

❖❖❖

Rocked in the Everlasting Arms

❖❖❖

THERE is a sense in which we are always children. In infancy we were rocked to sleep in the loving arms of our mother. In similar manner we may be enfolded all our life long in the loving arms of God. He said, "As one whom his mother comforteth, so will I comfort you." (Isaiah 66:13.)

The Bible tells us that the essence of genius is to be as a little child. That means to have the attitude of trust, to demonstrate confidence, to live joyfully, to enter wholeheartedly into life; in other words, to be a normal, natural, happy person. It means to live and work with relaxed power. It also means to have the ability when night-time comes to lie down and sleep like a child in complete relaxation and naturalness.

Jesus knew how to relax, for once in a storm His disciples saw Him lying sound asleep in the stern of the boat—"rocked in the cradle of the deep." Upon noting their tension, He told them that faith would calm the storms that frighten them, and that they, even as He, might meet life in quiet confidence.

There is an instinctive and normal mother attachment in each of us. No matter how old we become, there is some holdover of the infantile state, which is the source of our longing for the quality of comfort a mother gives. An adult person cannot be rocked to sleep in a mother's arms. So one of the subtlest of all mechanisms was devised, the transference from mother's arms to God's arms.

A profound secret of rest is to conceive imaginatively that His everlasting arms are under and around you, sustaining, protecting and comforting. This sense of Divine support and love is essential to relaxation in its deepest meaning.

I once knew a great artist, a very famous man whose skill is celebrated in the annals of painting. He was a large man physically, and radiated gusto and the joy of living. With all of his superb intellectual and notable scholarship, he had a childlike attitude toward God. "I have the time of my life all my life," he declared. "Every dawn is a new thrill; every sunset a fresh delight. And when at night I lie down to sleep, the dear Lord just puts His arm around me and soothes me into slumber." This man's boundless energy was drawn from the depths of a simple yet profound faith.

Do not be ashamed to be as a child in your relationship to God. Let the everlasting arms rock you to sleep. In complete trust, relax on God's amazing kindliness. He will take care of you day and night, forever.

"Ye shall find rest for your souls." (Jeremiah 6:16.)

"Cast thy burden upon the Lord, and he shall sustain thee." (Psalm 55:22.)

PART SIX
The "How" Cards

O̲v̲e̲r̲ the years I have discovered that many people, and I am tempted to say most people, face the same difficulties in life, although each one takes its individual form.

To solve these problems and overcome these difficulties I have worked out certain techniques. They are given in the ten "How" Cards which follow. These are for reference during spare moments of the day whenever you are trying to settle, once and for all, one of these perplexing problems of living.

The ten patterns in which these questions repeatedly appear to me may be described as follows:

First, confusion. Many people seem to be bewildered because life is full of anxieties, success leads only to increased responsibility, nothing ever seems permanently settled and peaceful. The reason they feel this way is that they have not faced up to the most fundamental question of all: HOW TO SOLVE A PROBLEM.

Second, occupation. All of us have to do something to fill the waking hours of our lives. Recreation and entertainment serve this purpose pleasantly for a time, but ultimately they pall. We need something to make us feel important. We should be thankful for the opportunity to work, whether it be running a machine, a business, or a house. Yet work is often a burden instead of a blessing. If this is your problem, give thought to the card: HOW TO MAKE YOUR WORK EASY.

Third, anxiety. Pollyanna may have been a most attractive child, but none of us can go through life being glad about everything. It is only when we live in a state of anxiety, without reaching a conclusion about anything, that it is time, as Hamlet thought, to "take arms against a sea of troubles." That is the purpose of HOW TO BREAK THE WORRY HABIT.

Fourth, tension. As I have remarked before in this book, this seems to be the malady characteristic of our times. To live in health, harmony and happiness it is essential to cultivate serenity. That is the technique described in HOW TO RELAX.

Fifth, self-confidence. This quality is akin to faith. With it, all things are possible; without it, almost nothing. If your experience leads you to believe that this may be a fault of your character, practise the precepts of HOW TO OVERCOME YOUR INFERIORITY COMPLEX.

Sixth, grief. This is real; it comes to everybody. There is no escaping it, but it can be endured with courage; it can even be an enrichening experience. How to find comfort in time of grief is described in HOW TO MEET SORROW.

Seventh, popularity. Most people, I think, could find many friends and pleasant companions if they would take the trouble to look for them and deserve them. How easy and pleasant it is to do this will appear from a study of HOW TO GET PEOPLE TO LIKE YOU.

Eighth, tolerance. Ill feelings toward others do them less harm than to ourselves. It may be that we have just cause for envy, malice or resentment, but if only for purely selfish reasons we should learn not to harbour these evil spirits. That is why it is so important to learn HOW TO FORGIVE.

Ninth, religion. Though many people attend the church of their faith regularly, whether from a sense of duty or a sincere desire to worship God, I wonder if they obtain the personal reward which such attendance should assure them.

It is not enough merely to attend divine services as a matter of habit. Religious worship can mean much more than this, and how it can do so is shown in HOW TO GO TO CHURCH.

Tenth, prayer. Just as many people fail to experience the real meaning of church attendance, so many say their prayers regularly, but by rote. To see whether it can add significance and happiness to your life, try following the principles given in HOW TO SAY YOUR PRAYERS.

Not all of these cards may be pertinent to your particular problems. But if one or more do apply, I am sure that using these cards will be as helpful to you as it has been to the many, many people who have tried them and found them effective.

HOW TO GO TO CHURCH

Ten Rules for Getting Effective Results from Church-going

First: Go regularly to church. A prescription ordered by a physician to be taken at regular intervals is not effective if taken once a year.

Second: Think of church-going as a skill governed by definite rules.

Third: Spend a quiet Saturday evening and get a good sleep. Get in condition for Sunday.

Fourth: Go in a relaxed state of body and mind. Don't rush to church. Go in a leisurely manner. The absence of tension is a requisite to successful worship.

Fifth: Go with the expectation of enjoyment. Church is not a gloomy place. Christianity is a radiant and happy way of living.

Sixth: Sit relaxed in the pew, feet on floor, hands loosely in lap or at sides. Allow the body to yield to the contour of the pew. Don't sit rigid. God's power cannot reach your personality through a tied-up body and mind.

Seventh: Go expecting to get your problem solved in church. Think hard during the week, but let the problem "simmer" in the mind on Sunday. In church conceive of God's peace as quieting your thoughts to permit insights from the depths to come to the surface of your mind.

Eighth: In church practise eliminating all ill will. Grudges block the flow of spiritual power. To cast out ill will pray in church for those against whom you feel resentful.

Ninth: Practise the art of meditation. Think of some beautiful and peaceful scene, perhaps even your favourite trout-stream. Then fix your mind on Christ. Think about God. This will tend to bring you peace and refreshment.

Tenth: Go to church expecting some great and exciting thing to happen to you. Every Sunday some people's lives become thrillingly different. It can happen to you.

HOW TO SAY YOUR PRAYERS

Ten Rules for Getting Effective Results from Prayer

First: Set aside a few minutes every day. Do not say anything. Simply practise thinking about God. This will make your mind spiritually receptive.

Second: Then pray orally, using simple, natural words. Tell God anything that is on your mind. Do not think you must use stereotyped pious phrases. Talk to God in your own language. He understands it.

Third: Pray as you go about the work of the day, on the subway or bus or at your desk. Utilise minute prayers by closing your eyes to shut out the world and concentrating on God's presence. The more you can do this every day the nearer you will feel God's presence.

Fourth: Do not always ask when you pray, but instead affirm that God's blessings are being given, and spend most of your prayers giving thanks.

Fifth: Pray with the belief that sincere prayers can reach out and surround your loved ones with God's love and protection.

Sixth: Never use a negative thought in prayer. Only positive thoughts get results.

Seventh: Always express willingness to accept God's will. Ask for what you want, but be willing to take what God gives you. It may be better than what you ask for.

Eighth: Practise the attitude of putting everything in God's hands. Ask for the ability to do your best and to leave the results confidently to God.

Ninth: Pray for people you do not like or who have mistreated you. Resentment is blockade number one of spiritual power.

Tenth: Make a list of people for whom to pray. The more you pray for other people, especially those not connected with you, and those who do not like you, the more prayer results will come back to you.

HOW TO SOLVE A PROBLEM

Ten Rules for Getting Answers to Everyday Perplexities

First: Believe that for every problem there is a solution.

Second: Keep calm. Tension blocks the flow of thought power. Your brain cannot operate efficiently under stress. Go at your problem easy-like though earnestly.

Third: Don't try to force an answer. Keep your mind relaxed so that the solution will open up and become clear.

Fourth: Assemble all the facts impartially, impersonally and judicially.

Fifth: List these facts on paper. This clarifies your thinking, bringing the various elements into orderly system. You see as well as think. Thus the problem becomes objective, not subjective.

Sixth: Pray about your problem, affirming that God will flash illumination into your mind.

Seventh: Believe in and seek God's guidance on the promise of the 73rd Psalm, "Thou wilt guide me by thy counsel."

Eighth: Trust the faculty of insight and intuition.

Ninth: Go to church and let your subconscious work on the problem as you attune to the mood of worship. Creative spiritual thinking has amazing power to give "right" answers.

Tenth: If you follow these nine steps faithfully, then the answer that develops in your mind, or comes to pass, is the right answer to your problem.

HOW TO MAKE YOUR WORK EASIER

Ten Rules for Taking the Hard Way Out of Your Job

First: Don't get the idea you are Atlas carrying the world on your shoulders. Don't strain so hard. Don't take yourself so seriously.

Second: Determine to like your work. Then it will become a pleasure, not drudgery. Perhaps you do not need to change your job. Change yourself and your work will seem different.

Third: Plan your work—work your plan. Lack of system produces that "I'm swamped" feeling.

Fourth: Don't try to do everything at once. That is why time is spread out. Heed that wise advice from the Bible, "This one thing I do."

Fifth: Get a correct mental attitude, remembering that ease or difficulty in your work depends upon how you think about it. Think it's hard and you make it hard. Think it's easy and it tends to become easier.

Sixth: Become efficient in your work. "Knowledge is power" (over your job). It is always easier to do a thing right.

Seventh: Practise being relaxed. Easy does it. Don't press or tug. Take it in your stride.

Eighth: Discipline yourself not to put off until tomorrow what you can do today. Accumulation of undone jobs makes your work harder. Keep your work up to schedule.

Ninth: Pray about your work. You will get relaxed efficiency by so doing.

Tenth: Take on the "unseen partner". It is surprising the load He will take off you. God is as much at home in offices, factories, stores, kitchens as in churches. He knows more about your job than you do. His help will make your work efficient.

HOW TO BREAK THE WORRY HABIT

Ten Rules for Curing the Greatest Malady

First: Know that worry is a habit, formed or broken like any habit.

Second: Realise worry is your enemy. The word means to choke. Worry has a most devastating effect on your personality. It is the greatest modern plague.

Third: Consider that worries usually fall into three percentage categories: 40 per cent of your worries are about the past; 50 per cent about the future; 10 per cent about present matters.

Fourth: To break the habit of worrying about past mistakes, practise the art of forgetting. Every morning and evening repeat this mental health statement, "Forgetting those things which are behind, and reaching forth unto those things which are before, I press toward the mark."

Fifth: Meditate on a wise statement by William James, the great psychologist: "The essence of genius is to know what to overlook" (to pass by, to forget) or in a modern slang phrase—"skip it".

Sixth: Every day affirm faith in your future—the world's future. Repeat the hymn line, "So long Thy power hath blest me, sure it still will lead me on."

Seventh: Practise the art of imperturbability. Whatever the stress, say, "God is keeping me calm and peaceful."

Eighth: Practise emptying the mind, affirming, "I am now emptying my mind of all anxiety, fear, insecurity."

Ninth: Practise filling the mind. Say, "God is now filling my mind with peace—with courage—with calm assurance."

Tenth: Practise God's presence affirming, "God is with me now. God is my constant companion. God will never leave me. I will never leave God."

HOW TO RELAX

Ten Rules for Losing Your Tension

First: Sprinkle one-minute quiet periods through the busiest part of your day. This will break the strain and keep you effective until the day's end.

Second: Get fifteen minutes of continuous quietness at some time during the day.

Third: During this quiet period use definite relaxation techniques. Physical, mental and spiritual discipline can reduce tension.

Fourth: Inhale and exhale three long breaths. Raise your arms and allow your hands to fall on your knees like a wet leaf on a log. What is more relaxed than a wet leaf on a log?

Fifth: Conceive of God's relaxing peace as touching, in turn, every muscle in your body and face, finally resting quietly upon your eyes.

Sixth: Relax the mind by imagination. Mentally you can take a trip without going away at all.

Seventh: In your imagination dwell for a moment upon the most peaceful and beautiful scenes you can visualise.

Eighth: By your thought attach your life to God's re-creative energy. Think of yourself as being renewed physically, emotionally and spiritually.

Ninth: Every day repeat each of the following statements three times: "Thou wilt keep him in perfect peace, whose mind is stayed on thee."—"Come unto me . . . and I will give you rest."—"Peace I give unto you." Then make these statements personal, inserting your name.

Tenth: "Drain" your mind of hate, impure thinking, dishonest desires and fears. These are the infection centres of tension. When they are drained off, relaxation becomes complete.

HOW TO OVERCOME YOUR INFERIORITY COMPLEX

Ten Rules for Getting Self-Confidence

First: Hold in your mind a picture of yourself succeeding. Your mind will seek to actualise this image.

Second: When a negative thought comes to mind deliberately cancel it with a positive thought.

Third: Do not build up obstacles in your imagination.

Fourth: Do not be awestruck by other people or try to copy them.

Fifth: Repeat ten times a day these words, "If God be for me who can be against me."

Sixth: Get a competent counsellor to help you understand the origin of your inferiority feeling which often begins in childhood. Self-knowledge leads to a cure.

Seventh: Ten times each day repeat aloud the following affirmation, "I can do all things through Christ which strengtheneth me." Conceive of yourself as receiving this strength.

Eighth: Realistically estimate your ability; then raise the estimate 10 per cent. Do not become egotistical, but develop a wholesome self-respect.

Ninth: Through prayer attach yourself to the flow of spiritual power.

Tenth: Believe that God is with you, for nothing can defeat that partnership.

HOW TO MEET SORROW

Ten Rules for Finding Comfort

First: Develop the philosophical realisation that certain inevitabilities exist in human experience. Learn to get along with the inevitable.

Second: Realise that every life has many phases from the cradle to the grave, each making its contribution to the sum total of your personality and wisdom. Sorrow is an important one of these phases and is part of God's arrangement.

Third: Consider that the manner in which you receive your sorrow will effect, for good or bad, your entire subsequent life.

Fourth: Realise that, difficult and painful as it is, you can reorganise and absorb the sorrowful experience and go on living. Human nature is endowed with an adjustable and resilient mechanism.

Fifth: Remind yourself that while death changes the circumstances of your association with your loved one, it does not separate you. Since "love can never lose its own" you will be conscious, in high moments, of your loved one's spiritual presence.

Sixth: When sorrow comes, give normal expression to it. Don't be ashamed of it or repress it.

Seventh: Go about your usual activities, do not avoid familiar scenes or places. Carry on right where you are, thus normalising the experience.

Eighth: Keep reminding yourself that your loved one is within the Father's house of many mansions and is surrounded by love and beauty.

Ninth: Reaffirm the great old faith of the Bible that you will meet again in that land that is "fairer than day" where there is no separation.

Tenth: Look for opportunities to give comfort and healing to other people. By helping to relieve their sorrow, your own will become easier to bear.

HOW TO GET PEOPLE TO LIKE YOU

Ten Rules for Getting the Esteem of Others

First: Learn to remember names. Inefficiency at this point may indicate that your interest is not sufficiently outgoing. A man's name is very important to him.

Second: Be a comfortable person so there is no strain in being with you—be an 'old shoe, old hat' kind of individual.

Third: Acquire the quality of relaxed easy-goingness so that things do not ruffle you.

Fourth: Don't be egotistical. Guard against giving the impression you know it all. Be natural and humble.

Fifth: Cultivate the quality of being stimulating and interesting so that people will want to be with you and get something from you.

Sixth: Study to get the scratchy elements, even those of which you may be unconscious, out of your personality. Expert counselling may help in this.

Seventh: Sincerely attempt to heal, on an honest Christian basis, every misunderstanding you have had or now have. Drain off your grievances.

Eighth: Definitely practise liking people until you learn to do so genuinely. Will Rogers said, "I never met a man I didn't like." Try to be that way.

Ninth: Never miss an opportunity to say a word of congratulation upon anyone's achievement, or express sympathy in sorrow or disappointment.

Tenth: Get a deep spiritual experience so that you have something to give to people that will help them to be stronger and meet life more effectively. They will love you for it.

HOW TO FORGIVE

Ten Rules for Ending Resentment

First: When anyone hurts you, put "spiritual iodine" on the wound at once. That is, pray hard about it. If you do not do this, it will fester.

Second: If resentment has hardened in your thoughts, apply grievance drainage. That is, open your mind and let the grievance flow out.

Third: Do this by unburdening yourself to a trusted counsellor or write a letter to the person against whom you have the resentment. Then tear it up and while holding the pieces in your hand pray for the person and forgive him.

Fourth: Become fully aware of the harm resentment can do you, even to making you ill. Think of that whenever a hate thought comes.

Fifth: Don't stop with forgiving a time or two. Do it, if necessary, seventy times seven—490 times to be literal.

Sixth: Thinking about forgiving is not enough. You must come to a specific moment when you say, "With God's help I *now* forgive (insert name of person)."

Seventh: Repeat the Lord's Prayer, inserting your offender's name, "Forgive *me my* trespasses as I forgive . . ."

Eighth: Pray for the other person, asking specific blessings for him, especially concerning matters which have previously annoyed you the most.

Ninth: Speak in a kindly and complimentary manner and as often as possible about the person against whom you harbour antagonism.

Tenth: Make a sincere study of the personality factors which created an unhappy relationship so that the "mistake pattern" in yourself may not recur.